TRAVELING WITH OUR STATE

NORTH CAROLINA
LIGHTHOUSES

A FIELD GUIDE TO OUR COASTAL LANDMARKS

Where to stay, what to eat, and how to make
the most of a lighthouse getaway

FROM

Our State
NORTH CAROLINA

GREENSBORO, N.C.

NORTH CAROLINA
LIGHTHOUSES

A FIELD GUIDE TO OUR COASTAL LANDMARKS

Where to stay, what to eat, and how to make
the most of a lighthouse getaway

Published by *Our State* magazine, Greensboro, N.C.

North Carolina's Lighthouses: A Field Guide to Our Coastal Landmarks
copyright © 2010 by *Our State* magazine.
All rights reserved.
Published by Mann Media Inc.
P.O. Box 4552, Greensboro, N.C. 27404
(800) 948-1409; www.ourstate.com
Printed in the United States by R.R. Donnelley

Lighthouse illustrations by Steven Noble

Library of Congress Control Number:
2010923073

NORTH CAROLINA
LIGHTHOUSES
A FIELD GUIDE TO OUR COASTAL LANDMARKS

TABLE OF CONTENTS

TABLE OF CONTENTS

INTRODUCTION
WHY WE NEED OUR LIGHTHOUSES

BY T. EDWARD NICKENS

Low in the dark, cool belly of Old Baldy, I can almost hear the century-old echoes of the lighthouse keeper's footsteps. I imagine him clad in pea coat and captain's cap, boot-shod and blowing hard, as he climbs the circular wooden stairway with fuel and flame — a bucket of whale oil in one hand and a lamp in the other.

A stiff breeze rattles through the lantern gallery above, swirling down the stairwell and tickling the flame of the lamp. His footfalls grow louder. Thomp. Thomp. Thomp.

Twilight falls across North Carolina's Cape Fear River as the keeper ascends. Shadows dance against the cement skin of the sloping lighthouse walls. The heavy sweet-slick smell of the whale oil is strong in the keeper's nose. Mounting the ladder onto the gallery, he sets the oil bucket on an overhead step. Before him the flat sheet of the black Atlantic spreads beneath early-rising stars. He touches his lamp to the lighthouse wick, and a flame flares up against the polished reflector to light a dark sea.

The sounds fade. A cold wind sweeps through the open lighthouse door. Midday light blasts through dirty panes of glass, and I walk to the window, crunching leaves of fallen plaster on the brick floor. The echoes die as I squint out into the sunlight.

IN THE OLDEN DAYS

In the beginning, there was probably a fire on a hill, a blaze built on some Mediterranean outcropping. As long as sailors have ventured beyond sight of land, they have needed beacons to guide them home or to warn them of unseen dangers below the waves. But when the sails of ships began to dip further below the horizon on more distant voyages, the small fire on the hill wasn't light enough. The notion of a lighthouse was born.

The first lighthouse we know about was the Pharaohs of Alexandria, built some 2,300 years ago — a 400-foot-tall white marble monolith near the ancient Egyptian port. It rose above a huge courtyard surrounded by lower-level galleries, arcades, and gardens. By day, the Pharaohs spewed pillars of smoke; by night its fires were reportedly visible for 30 miles. One of the Seven Wonders of the Ancient World, this venerable lighthouse stood for 1,600 years before an earthquake toppled it.

When the French started building the Tour de Cordouan in the Bay of Biscay in 1584, they combined the Egyptian lighthouse idea with their own

> "When the sails of ships began to dip further below the horizon on more distant voyages, the small fire on the hill wasn't light enough. The notion of a lighthouse was born."

> We may not need lighthouses now the way we used to, but we still need what they stand for — a reference point between our world and the other world that lies beyond the breakers.

innovations. Upon completion 26 years later, the lighthouse boasted two lantern rooms, two chambers handsomely fitted for visits by the king, and a third-story chapel with a domed ceiling.

SEVEN SENTINELS

A visitor will find no such luxuries in the lighthouses of the North Carolina coast. Rising from the low, sandy barrier islands that form the fragile eastern edge of the Mid-Atlantic, the seven lighthouses still standing here are largely unadorned structures. No formal chambers, no columns, or courtyards embellish them. What little ornamentation there is — painted stripes, checks, and spiral patterns — is more utilitarian than aesthetic.

These beacons were built to warn of shifting bars and killing shoals, those ridges of sand that lurk beneath the surface for miles out to sea. By night, the warnings were carried by the flash of the lighthouse beacon; by day, distinctive paint patterns marked the Diamond or Frying Pan Shoals or the turbulent waters where rivers of currents collided.

But for all their stark design and purpose, North Carolina's seven surviving sentinels — at Currituck Beach, Bodie Island, Cape Hatteras, Ocracoke Island, Cape Lookout, Oak Island, and Bald Head — have today become symbols of the Tar Heel coast as distinctive as sea oats and Scotch Bonnets.

Lighthouses are no longer the sole link between men on land and men at sea; their function is now largely performed by radar, sonar, and loran. But these high-tech guides have yet to displace the lighthouse as totems of our seafaring past. We may not need lighthouses now the way we used to, but we still need what they stand for — a reference point between our world and the other world that lies beyond the breakers.

Today, no lighthouse keepers remain to haul oil and flame to the lantern galleries of the Carolina sentinels. Thousand-watt bulbs blast their beams automatically as far as18 miles across the sea, as each lighthouse flashes its own signature code. The United States Coast Guard periodically checks the lighthouses, cleaning the lenses and replacing the bulbs, but no one lives in them. No longer are these masonry monoliths lone outposts of civilization on the outer edge of the world.

Still, on clear coastal nights, when the flash of a lamp arcs across the black horizon, it is not so difficult to imagine those days long ago. The same tides pull at the same frail isles, the same shoals lie hidden under the blank face of the Atlantic. And, as in the past, people are still drawn to these North Carolina landmarks — if not to their light, then to the history they illuminate.

CURRITUCK
LIGHTHOUSE

IN THE AREA: DUCK,
COROLLA,
KITTY HAWK

CHAPTER ONE

CURRITUCK BEACH LIGHTHOUSE

RED-BRICK BEAUTY

I T TOOK ABOUT A MILLION RED BRICKS to build the Currituck Beach Lighthouse, giving North Carolina's northernmost beacon its distinctive color. "We're the last mortar lighthouse built on the coast of North Carolina," says site manager Meghan Agresto. "We're also the only one left unpainted on the east coast of North Carolina, so it makes it really special and very pretty."

When the first-order Fresnel lens was lit on December 1, 1875, the tower illuminated the remaining stretch of dark coastline between the lighthouses at Cape Henry, Virginia, and Bodie Island. Today, that same lens remains in operation, still flashing in distinctive 20-second intervals that can be seen for 19 nautical miles.

Connie Mason, an award-winning folklorist and the maritime heritage officer with the North Carolina Department of Commerce, says the earthquake that devastated Charleston, South Carolina, on the night of August 31, 1886, was felt in Corolla and caused cracks to form in the mortar

HOW TO GET HERE:
At the junction of U.S. Highway 158 and N.C. Highway 12, take N.C. Highway 12 heading north toward Duck and Corolla. The lighthouse entrance is 20 miles from the junction, on the left, just beyond the Currituck Heritage Park sign.

of the lighthouse. "The story goes that the lightkeeper's wife was going up the stairs with her baby," Mason says. "She fell down the steps and got hurt."

In 1980, the Currituck Beach light station was taken over by the nonprofit group, Outer Banks Conservationists. The lighthouse and the adjacent lighthouse keepers' quarters have undergone a major restoration. Visitors to the site can climb 214 steps to the top and visit the Victorian-era keepers' house known for its "stick-style" design (featuring flat-board banding and other applied, geometric-patterned ornamentation).

"People who see photographs of what the keepers' house used to look like are amazed at the way it looks now," Agresto says. "Now it looks exactly like it did in photographs we have from 1892. It's fantastic that concerned citizens can get together and make a change like this." — *Misti Lee*

CLIMBING CURRITUCK
WALK IN HISTORY'S FOOTSTEPS

Yes, you'll squeeze into a tight, winding staircase, and you'll climb 214 leg-quivering steps to reach the top of the Currituck Beach Lighthouse. But the view from the lighthouse gallery just below the lantern room is worth it. Admission is $7 to enter the lighthouse. Take a deep breath, and begin your ascent: There are nine sturdy platform landings where you can stop for a rest before taking on the next set of stairs.

STAY AND SLEEP

THE SANDERLING RESORT & SPA

Art lovers flock to this world-class resort, renowned for its collection as much as for its spectacular setting.

THE SANDERLING RESORT & SPA
1461 Duck Road, Duck, N.C. 27949
phone: (252) 261-4111 or (800) 701-4111 *web:* thesanderling.com

WHEN THE SANDERLING RESORT AND SPA opened its doors in 1985, its then-remote location on the Outer Banks may have seemed an unlikely spot for a luxury inn. But with a simple serenity and a nod to nature evident in every aspect of the resort's decor, The Sanderling is just what many vacationers have in mind when seeking a place to relax and recharge.

The 12-acre property, which stretches from sea to sound, is now home to a cluster of buildings: Three inns house 88 guest rooms and suites, each one decorated in restful neutral tones and soft shades of sea-glass blues and greens and featuring large baths with walk-in showers and soaking tubs, granite counters, and bronze-finished lighting fixtures. An eclectic mix of wood furnishings and wicker touches add to the feel of comfortable elegance.

> Just what vacationers have in mind when seeking a place to relax and recharge.

One of the hallmarks of The Sanderling's decor is its art collection, a fabulous array of works reflecting the natural world. The resort's owners, a Winston-Salem couple who cherish their privacy, began installing pieces from their personal collection when they opened The Sanderling. The art on display ranges from life-size sculptures of birds in wood and bronze to framed Hermès and Gucci silk scarves depicting flora and fauna to exquisite porcelain birds and fish designed by artisans from the Royal Worcester, Boehm, and Lorenz Hutschenreuther studios.

The Sanderling also features the largest private collection of works by renowned artist Grainger McKoy, who sculpts birds in wood, bronze, and sterling silver. Considered by some to be a modern-day John James Audubon in his depiction of the avian world, McKoy has exhibited at the American Museum of Natural History in New York City, the Royal Ontario Museum, the Brandywine River Museum in Pennsylvania, and Brookgreen Gardens in South Carolina.

Among the many McKoy pieces found throughout the resort, his impressive "Covey Rise," a depiction of quail being flushed from a thicket of grass, is the centerpiece of the Main Inn's Grand Gallery. This limited edition piece, completed by McKoy in 1981, is also in the private collections of former President Jimmy Carter, former First Lady Nancy Reagan, and actor Bruce Willis.

On the gallery's second level, McKoy's gravity-defying piece "Sanderlings in Flight" is the main attraction. Fifteen birds, carved of basswood, brush wingtips as they seem to skim across water carved out of black walnut.

> "We knew that this art would add a lot to our setting on the North Carolina coast."

"Grainger's art fits in so well at The Sanderling," says the resort's owner, "so we kept adding pieces over the years. Right from the beginning, we knew that this art would add a lot to our setting on the North Carolina coast."

The Sanderling is also home to 18 original Audubon prints, including the "Great Blue Heron," the "Brown Pelican," and the "Common American Swan," which grace the Main Inn.

It's the "Doughty Birds," porcelain representations of birds created by Dorothy Doughty that are the artistic highlight of the resort. Doughty, a well-known English artist, designed a collection of "Birds of North America" for the Royal Worcester porcelain company from the 1930s until her death in the 1960s. More than two dozen of Doughty's American birds are on display at the inn's gourmet restaurant, The Left Bank. Some are quite rare, including the representation of a pair of quail; just 12 of the porcelain sculptures of quail were ever made. — *Katherine Kopp*

FLY A KITE

Gliders — here's your place to take wing.

KITTY HAWK KITES

Several retail locations are located along the Outer Banks, from Corolla to Ocracoke. Hang gliding is available only at Jockey's Ridge, but you can shop for kiteboarding and surfing equipment at any of the Kitty Hawk Kites shops.

phone: (877) 359-8447 **web:** kittyhawk.com

O N THE OUTER BANKS, THE WRIGHT BROTHERS' story is well known. But there's another story grounded in this area, that of Francis and Gertrude Rogallo. In the late 1940s, Francis, an engineer for the National Advisory Committee for Aeronautics in Hampton, Virginia, came up with the idea for a simple, practical aircraft for sport and recreation. Francis enlisted the help of his wife, Gertrude, and the two used curtains from their home to construct a flexible wing based on models he had tested in a homemade wind tunnel (the wind came from an industrial-size floor fan).

On August 15, 1948, the Rogallos came to Jockey's Ridge and successfully flew their cloth wing, christening it the Flexi-Kite. In the 1960s, the Rogallo wing developed into an inexpensive, foot-launchable glider. The couple allowed their design to be copied freely in order to promote the new sport, and, in 1971, adventurous types gathered for the world's first hang glider event in California.

You don't have to go west to go aloft. Since 1974, Kitty Hawk Kites has instructed more than 300,000 people on how to experience personal flight. From the Jockey's Ridge location, you'll venture up, in tandem with an instructor, 2,000 feet above the sandy dunes of the Outer Banks. After the ultra-light tow plane disconnects, you and your instructor glide with the wind as gracefully as a gull back down to terra firma. Stop in at any of the Kitty Hawk Kite locations along the Outer Banks to outfit your vacation with a kiteboard or surfboard. — *Bryan Oesterreich*

EXPLORE

COROLLA WILD HORSE MUSEUM

Fifty years after classes ended, the former Corolla Schoolhouse now serves as a museum dedicated to the area's wild horses.

COROLLA WILD HORSE MUSEUM/COROLLA SCHOOLHOUSE
1126 Old Schoolhouse Lane, Corolla, N.C. 27927
phone: (252) 453-8002 *web:* corollawildhorses.com

HOURS/ADMISSION
Summer hours: Monday-Saturday, 10 a.m.-4 p.m. (In the off-season, call ahead for hours of operation.) Admission is free.

MOST OF THE OLD ONE-ROOM SCHOOLHOUSES that once dotted the Outer Banks are long gone, but a tiny schoolhouse building in Corolla, 50 years after it closed as a school, is back on duty, revived as the Corolla Wild Horse Museum and the home base for the Corolla Wild Horse Fund, a nonprofit group that manages the herd.

The cheerful Corolla Schoolhouse sits in the heart of historic Corolla Village, a small pocket of the Outer Banks that, miraculously, has retained the character of its distant past — unpaved roads, historic clapboard buildings, and all. Village residents built the Corolla Schoolhouse around the turn of the 20th century, partly with materials that were salvaged from the beach; during the restoration, huge ship's timbers were discovered in the foundation. The dwindling population of Corolla led to the school's closing in 1958; in 1999, local preservationists Doug and Sharon Twiddy began the restoration of the structure that had been empty for nearly 50 years.

Doug Twiddy, owner of a northern Outer Banks

SUMMER FUN
In the summer, on Tuesdays from 11 a.m. to 2 p.m., the museum offers children's painting parties. Each child paints a wooden cutout of a horse, and then the horse cutouts are hung in the trees in the front yard of the schoolhouse for the rest of the week.

real estate company, has a passion for historic preservation. His first restoration project was the Kill Devil Hills Lifesaving Station, along with several other buildings in Corolla Village. The Twiddys renovated the Corolla Schoolhouse in 1999 with a different intention.

"We had this space, and we wanted to use it to teach, but we didn't know what to teach," says Twiddy. "Then it occurred to me that one of the most-asked questions in Corolla is about the wild horses, and that was our answer. We decided to use the schoolhouse as a wild horse museum."

While the Corolla wild horses once wandered freely through the area, today the horses roam a 12,000-acre stretch of federal, state, and private land that is fenced in on the north and south to prevent them from straying back into Corolla or over the state line into Virginia.

The resulting museum is a fun educational experience about the horses and provides a glimpse into the days of the one-room schoolhouse.

Upon stepping in the schoolhouse door, the small room with its worn pine floors takes you back in time, but the giant photographic images of horses grab your attention. A video about the Corolla wild horses, narrated by Charles Kuralt, runs continuously. One exhibit has a button to push to hear the horses whinny, nicker, neigh, snort, and squeal. Another exhibit teaches about the colors of the wild horses — bay, chestnut, paint, black, and flaxen mane and tail. There's a horse's leg bone to study and aerial photos showing the horses' current habitat. A volunteer is always available to answer questions.

> "One of the most-asked questions in Corolla is about the wild horses ..."

The Twiddys ran the horse museum privately for two years but struggled to make it work financially. A few years ago, Sharon approached the Corolla Wild Horse Fund to see if they had a need for the horse exhibits. At that time, the Horse Fund happened to be looking for new office space; in a happy arrangement, Currituck County now leases the Corolla Schoolhouse for the Horse Fund, and, in turn, the Horse Fund operates the Corolla Wild Horse Museum in the front room.

It's a partnership that has kept the museum open to the public and, even more important, brought much-needed public awareness to the efforts of the Corolla Wild Horse Fund. — *Molly Harrison*

ISLAND BOOKSTORE

Beachcomb for literary treasure on the Outer Banks.

ISLAND BOOKSTORE (THREE LOCATIONS)
1177 Duck Road, Duck, N.C. 27949
phone: (252) 261-8981 *web:* islandbooksobx.com

1130 Corolla Village Road, Corolla, N.C. 27929
phone: (252) 453-2292

3712 North Croatan Hightway, Kitty Hawk, N.C. 27949
phone: (252) 255-5590

I N THE DUCK BRANCH OF THE ISLAND BOOKSTORE, a framed quote by historian Barbara Tuchman seems apt. "Books," she says, "are engines of change, windows on the world, and lighthouses erected in the sea of time."

"Some might consider that we're on the edge of the world in the middle of nowhere, but we pride ourselves on offering a selection of books to rival stores in any major city," says Bill Rickman, who owns the shops with his wife, Ursula.

Visits by authors are special occasions, and the Rickmans' customers display a remarkable diversity of interests. "We always glow a little," Ursula says, "when customers from [Washington] D.C. and Philadelphia [Pennsylvania] tell us they wait until their vacations each year to stock up on books from our stores."

They take special delight in selling books to vacationing children. "Their excitement for good reading is exhilarating," Ursula says. "It's a multigenerational reward and a pretty good prospect for the future of the book."— *Charles Blackburn*

DINER DINING

Take a seat in the 1939 Kullman dining car for a made-from-scratch meal.

KILL DEVIL GRILL
Milepost 9 3/4, N.C. Highway 12, Kill Devil Hills, N.C. 27948
phone: (252) 449-8181 *web:* thekilldevilgrill.com

HOURS
Lunch and dinner, Tuesday-Saturday, brunch on Sundays.

KILL DEVIL GRILL IS HOPPING — the seats are filled, the grill is sizzling, the jazz is swinging, the conversations are buzzing, and the waitresses are whizzing by with armloads of plates.

On a restaurant-scouting trip to the Outer Banks in 2002, Bill Tucker, who had been working as an area director for six restaurants in Washington, D.C., happened upon an interesting little nugget on the beach road in Kill Devil Hills — a 1939 Kullman diner car and restaurant. Formerly Millie's Diner, the car was listed on the National Register of Historic Places and meticulously restored but empty for the previous three years. With stainless-steel trim, rounded glass-block corners, painted metal siding, and Art Deco details outside, plus Formica-topped tables, a classic lunch counter, black-and-white tile floor, and red and stainless-steel stools inside, the diner was a classic brimming with hip, vintage appeal. Tucker bought it, packed up his belongings in D.C., and moved to Kill Devil Hills.

The menu is well-rounded but purposefully restrained, which gives Tucker and his kitchen staff the most creative leeway on the chalkboard specials, usually five per shift. You'll find local organic produce from nearby farmers and seafood from local waters, like Colington soft-shell crabs or local flounder or rockfish, or Gulf Stream tuna, mahimahi, and wahoo. "I keep it simple because I want to do everything well consistently with a smile," says Tucker. — *Molly Harrison*

JOHN'S DRIVE-IN

Slow down and enjoy the fast food at this coastal favorite that proves the best fun in the sun can be found off the sand.

JOHN'S DRIVE-IN
3716 North Virginia Dare Trail, Kitty Hawk, N.C. 27949
phone: (252) 261-6227

THIRTY-ONE YEARS OLD AND ABSOLUTELY LOVED by Outer Bankers, John's is a Kitty Hawk institution. Favorites here are the dolphin sandwich and the dolphin boat. John's flash-fries mahimahi in a light batter resulting in a succulent crisp coating around moist, flaky fish. The "boat" features mahimahi in a basket with fries. For the sandwich, a thick mahimahi fillet is stuffed into a hoagie roll with tartar or cocktail sauce and lettuce and tomato.

John's freshly made tuna salad is so popular they sell out of it nearly everyday. And there's The Big John, an Italian sub, along with burgers, hot dogs, crab cake sandwiches, and fried clams. But John's "create-your-own milkshakes" are the biggest draw. John's mixes in fruit, candy, chocolate, and butterscotch, and you'll often hear Outer Bankers raving about their favorite John's concoction: strawberry-Oreo, banana-chocolate-peanut butter, blueberry-peach.

John's has been operated by the Tice family since 1977. John Tice Sr., who started the business, has passed away, but his son, John Tice Jr., and his family continue to run the business, much to the delight of its loyal followers. Tice Jr. is on site every day, hand-preparing most of the dishes and cooking nearly 90 percent of the orders that come in the window. "That's the way my mom and dad did it, and I'm just keeping it going," he says. "We're a small, family-owned place. We take care of the kids and the dogs and families. We don't change." — *Molly Harrison*

THE SNOWBIRD

Generations of beachgoers remember burgers and fries — and especially ice cream — at this institution that's been serving for a half-century.

THE SNOWBIRD
3530 South Virginia Dare Trail, Nags Head, N.C. 27959
phone: (252) 480-0000

WANCHESE NATIVE HELEN TILLETT STOKELY and her husband, Marvin, started The Snowbird in Norfolk, Virginia, in the late 1940s, but the Stokelys sold all their restaurant equipment to Mickey Daniels of Wanchese in the 1950s. Daniels kept the name when he opened the ice cream shop in Nags Head. When U.S. Highway 158 was built in Nags Head in the late 1950s, Daniels had to move his restaurant out of the way, selling it to his sister, Doll Gray. Gray and her husband, Walter, reopened at a new location along the Beach Road.

"People loved it," Gray remembers. "They came from everywhere and lined up all the way to the street for our ice cream." The specialty of the house was The Purple Cow, a combination of vanilla ice cream and NuGrape soda.

The restaurant changed hands a few times over the years, and these days, Scott Blumenthal and Jonathan Conwell have been carrying on The Snowbird legacy for the past six summers. "We've kept the old-school flavor of what a beach restaurant should be and added a new twist," says Blumenthal. In addition to regular and gourmet burgers and fries, The Snowbird offers its signature mahimahi Philly — a flash-fried fillet finished on the grill with peppers, onions, and cheese. They also serve sides of veggies and fruit.

Vacationers still flock to The Snowbird for ice cream, especially in the early evening, and for good reason: No fewer than 100 flavors of soft-serve are available. — *Molly Harrison*

BODIE
ISLAND
LIGHTHOUSE

**IN THE AREA:
MANTEO, NAGS HEAD**

CHAPTER TWO
BODIE ISLAND LIGHTHOUSE
HORIZONTAL HIGH-RISE

VISITORS TO THE BODIE ISLAND LIGHTHOUSE can let their minds wander back to 1872, when the black-and-white horizontally striped light station was built, filling in a dark 80-mile gap between the Currituck Beach Lighthouse and Hatteras Lighthouse.

"The light station is about a mile off the road, and when you go there, you can feel the history in the area," says Marcia Lyons, district interpreter at the Cape Hatteras National Seashore. "There aren't a lot of modern things. We have the parking lot and so forth, but it still looks much like it did. You can really imagine this isolated light station."

The lighthouse's first-order Fresnel lens was lit in 1872. The light was electrified in 1932, and its light pattern can be seen for 19 nautical miles, flashing over both Pamlico Sound and the Atlantic Ocean.

"The Bodie Lighthouse is not right smack on the ocean, and people wonder why it's so far from the ocean," Lyons says. "When they built it, it was closer

HOW TO GET HERE:

- The lighthouse is located about eight miles south of the U.S. Highway 158 and U.S. Highway 64 intersection.
- Upon reaching the Outer Banks on U.S. Highway 264, turn south on N.C. Highway 12 and enter the Cape Hatteras National Seashore. The road leading to the Bodie Island Lighthouse will be on your right after about six miles.
- A visitor center in the keeper's house is open daily from 9 a.m. to 6 p.m. from Memorial Day through Labor Day, and from 9 a.m. to 5 p.m. the rest of the year.
- The grounds around the lighthouse are accessible during daylight hours, and the base of the tower is open during the summer on Tuesdays, Wednesdays, and Thursdays. **For more information, call (252) 441-5711.**

to the inlet, but the inlet has migrated three miles [away] since it was broken through in the 1840s."

The first lighthouse on Bodie Island was built in 1848 but was abandoned after the 54-foot tower began to lean. A second, taller lighthouse was completed in 1858, but it didn't survive, either.

"That lighthouse was blown up by the Confederates during the Civil War so the Union couldn't use it," Lyons says. "Both the earlier lights were on the south side of the inlet that is now known as Pea Island Wildlife Refuge, so when they built the third one, it was built on the north side of the inlet, and that's where it stands now." — *Misti Lee*

HOW DID BODIE ISLAND GET THAT NAME?

POPULAR FOLKLORE attributes the name, which is pronounced "body" by the locals, to the many bodies that were found washed ashore from the abundance of shipwrecks in the area, fittingly foreboding for a region known as the "Graveyard of the Atlantic."

But the most likely explanation is found inside the lighthouse, on a plaque that bears the name "Body." According to Doug Stover, historian for the Outer Banks Group of the National Park Service, the original reference was "Body's" or "Boddy's" Island, indicating the name of the family who owned the land on which the lighthouse was built or of one of the men who helped to build the original structure.

STAY AND SLEEP

THE ROANOKE ISLAND INN

Experience the island tradition of down-home hospitality.

THE ROANOKE ISLAND INN
305 Fernando Street, Manteo, N.C. 27954
phone: (877) 473-5511 *web:* roanokeislandinn.com

IN THE 1860S, ASA AND MARTHA ANN CREEF JONES BUILT their home in Manteo, raised 10 children, and opened their home to the crews of showboats and mail boats coming ashore. Today, descendant Elizabeth Creef-Blizzard, innkeeper and general manager of the Roanoke Island Inn, keeps the family tradition going. For eight months each year, Creek-Blizzard opens rooms for guests, just as her ancestors did for generations. "We want you to feel like a special visitor in a private island house," she says.

> **Bikes offer guests a pleasant way to get acquainted with the island.**

From its white picket fence punctuated with roses to the koi pond in the quiet backyard, this inn feels like a home. Upon arrival, guests enter a greeting room, where they'll find an innkeeper's pantry stocked with snacks and game table and books surrounding a fireplace. Bikes wait in back of the inn, offering guests a pleasant way to get acquainted with the island.

After breakfast, visitors may opt for a stroll on the boardwalk, which will lead them past the George Washington Creef Boathouse featuring local shad boats and toward the reconstructed Roanoke Marshes lighthouse. Then it's on to the village to explore a variety of shops and restaurants. After dinner, guests fix a cup of coffee or tea in the innkeepers' pantry and head out to the best seat in the house — the second-story porch, where bullfrogs, insects, and other night critters provide background music for the scene in front of The Roanoke. — *Lynn Seldon*

STAY AND SLEEP

THE WHITE DOE INN

Named for the legend surrounding colonist Virginia Dare, the White Doe Inn is a getaway gem on Roanoke Island.

WHITE DOE INN
319 Sir Walter Raleigh Street, Manteo, N.C. 27954
phone: (800) 473-6091 *web:* whitedoeinn.com

IN 1898, A YEAR BEFORE MANO was incorporated as a town, local politician and businessman Theodore Meekins built a modest one-and-a-half story home on the eastern side of Roanoke Island. Meekins' wife, Rosa, however, saw a picture of a charming Queen Anne Victorian house in a catalog and just had to have it. Rather than moving or tearing down a perfectly good house, in 1910, Theodore added a three-story rendition of Rosa's dream house to the original structure.

The house was one of the most prominent in Manteo, and it remained in the Meekins family for eight decades. BeBe Woody, who had grown up on Roanoke Island, would often walk by the Meekins house as a child. "It was a magical place that little girls dream of someday living in," she says. Then, in the early 1990s, the house was put up for sale by John Meekins, nephew of Theodore Meekins Jr. At the same time, Woody

> "It was a magical place that little girls dream of someday living in."

and her husband, Bob, were in the process of retiring from the National Park Service and were looking for a new challenge. The inn filled that need.

Much work had to be done to transform the home into a bed and breakfast and to reclaim the elegance of the house's earlier years, but the Woodys' labor of love paid off. The former Theodore Meekins House opened in 1994, with the name White Doe Inn. The Woodys chose the name based on a local legend about Virginia Dare, who, according to the tale, was raised by the

Croatan Indians and was turned into a white doe by a bitter medicine man who could not claim her for his own because she loved another. "Virginia Dare has always represented beauty, mystery, and a new beginning for this area," says Woody. "The legend of the White Doe brings all this together in a great love story." — *L.A. Jackson*

PLAY

COQUINA BEACH

Lose yourself along this less-traveled expanse of beach.

COQUINA BEACH
Eight miles south of U.S. Highway 158 Nags Head, N.C. 27959

A PEACEFUL STRETCH OF SEASHORE, Coquina Beach at Bodie Island is considered one of the safest swimming beaches in the area. Along with enjoying the fun in the surf, visitors can take advantage of a variety of historical and natural programs and activities offered by the National Park Service, such as evening campfires in the summer and viewing the shipwrecked remains of the *Laura A. Barnes*, a schooner that came ashore in 1921. And if you just want to relax and dig your toes in the sand, look for some friendly companions: Coquina Beach got its name from the abundance of coquina clams that burrow in the sand here. — *Elizabeth Hudson*

JOCKEY'S RIDGE STATE PARK

The tallest natural sand dune in the eastern United States rewards hikers
with awesome views.

JOCKEY'S RIDGE STATE PARK
Milepost 12, U.S. Highway 158, Nags Head, N.C. 27959
phone: (252) 441-7132 *web:* jockeysridgestatepark.com

J OCKEY'S RIDGE CAPTURES THE IMAGINATION like few other
natural formations in North Carolina. Upon this magnificent, moving
pile of sand, people learn to hang glide; others perfect their sandboarding
skills. Most of us, however, challenge ourselves with a climb to the top
of the massive dune.

Before ascending the big mound, however, hone your sand-shuffling skills
on the Tracks in the Sand Trail. An out-and-back jaunt with a loop at the
end, this trail takes you across a sea of sand. (Park officials estimate that 30
million tons of sand compose the dune.)

The trail takes you across a sea of sand.

As you climb the ridges at posts 2 and 5, you
may feel as if you're trying to walk up a down
escalator. But don't give up. In addition to vistas
stretching for miles, Jockey's Ridge harbors a
host of wildlife — gray fox, deer, rabbits, birds, and possum — which leave
distinct tracks across the sand.

If you master the art of sand-shuffling and want more, veer right as you
near posts 5 and 4 on the return trip to ascend the apex of Jockey's Ridge
for well-earned, long-distance views. After conquering this crest, you'll find
some easier walking along a paved portion of the Mountains-to-Sea Trail
(on the left side of the pavilion), which weaves through the park, across the
parking area, and up to the entrance gate. — *Lynn Setzer*

MANTEO BOOKSELLERS
Beach lovers and book lovers go hand-in-hand
at the popular independent shop.

MANTEO BOOKSELLERS
105 Sir Walter Raleigh Street, Manteo, N.C. 27954
phone: (252) 473-1221 or (866) 473-1222 *web:* manteobooksellers.com
HOURS: Monday-Saturday, 10 a.m.-6 p.m. (summer hours; call for winter hours.)

LOCATED IN A QUAINT ELIZABETHAN-STYLE BUILDING on Sir Walter Raleigh Street, Manteo Booksellers looks like it might have been transplanted directly from merry old England. In fact, it's not far from where English colonists first landed on Roanoke Island in 1587. This is no ordinary bookshop. Its Old World charm casts a spell, inviting visitors to linger.

Steve Brumfield had never heard of the Outer Banks before coming to Manteo at the behest of a local businessman who wanted to start a bookshop and needed somebody to run it.

"I had been working for several years in a university town bookshop in the center of Washington state," Brumfield says. "In my dreams I hoped someday to open a bookshop."

After moving here, he and his sister later bought Manteo Booksellers. Getting a chance to meet visiting authors and talk to them about their work has been among the joys of the trade. He also learns a lot from his customers. "They tend to love music, art, and food, and share so much more beyond literature." Many return year after year as a traditional part of their beach trips, and it's easy to see why. Comfortable armchairs, soothing classical music, and a broad selection of titles combine for a memorable experience.

Among the whimsical bookshop events is Herbert Hoover Day, celebrated each August 10 on the former President's birthday. Partygoers drink "Herbert Sherbet Punch" and learn little-known presidential facts. — *Charles Blackburn*

EAT AND DRINK

OWENS' RESTAURANT

A multi-generational, family-operated eatery renowned for its crab crakes and hush puppies has become an Outer Banks institution.

OWENS' RESTAURANT
Milepost 16 1/2, Beach Road, Nags Head, N.C. 27959
phone: (252) 441-7309 *web:* owensrestaurant.com

WHEN OWENS' CAFE OPENED in Nags Head in 1946, the restaurant stayed closed for nine months and open only for the short tourist season: mid-May to the day after Labor Day. Back then, Owens' was a 24-seat cafe that served three meals a day and was one of few commercial establishments on the bald strip of sand in Nags Head.

Roanoke Island residents thought Bob and Clara Owens had lost their minds when they decided to move their restaurant from the Manteo waterfront, where they had started out in 1933, to the apparent nothingness of Nags Head. "What a huge step they took," says Clara Mae Owens Shannon, daughter of Bob and Clara. "I've often thought about the risk they took."

CLARA AT THE HELM

It proved a risk worth taking. With the addition of cottages and a small oceanfront motel, Owens' Cafe and Motel thrived in the summer. The cottages were full, and the restaurant was busy as word got around about Clara's hushpuppies, crab cakes, and fried fish.

Bob died in 1950, but Clara was determined to keep the business running on her own. Clara, who was known as "Miss O," established successful relationships with the local fishermen, and she was a known stickler for freshness. Her expertise in the kitchen was of great renown.

By the 1970s, a second generation was running Owens' Restaurant when Clara Mae and her husband, Lionel, along with Clara Mae's brother, Bobby and his wife, Sarah, began logging more hours. But Clara still had the reigns.

Even when she was elderly, Clara came to the restaurant in her wheelchair to make the crab cakes and the hushpuppy mix, and that was the very thing she did on the morning of the day she died.

Today, Clara Mae and Lionel, along with their daughter, Peaches, and her husband, Jim Eckhardt, run the show at Owens' Restaurant, although Clara Mae and Lionel say they seek counsel from the rest of the family often. The fourth generation, Peaches's 11-year-old son, Leo, is starting to help out at the restaurant, too.

Today, Owens' Restaurant is a 260-seat establishment that is constantly filled to capacity and has a lengthy roster of loyal customers, some of whom still remember dining at Owens' Cafe on the Manteo waterfront in the 1930s and early '40s. It's not at all a stretch to classify this restaurant as an Outer Banks institution.

> "Coming to Owens' is like coming home."

"Coming to Owens' is like coming home," is something Clara Mae says she hears from customers all the time. "That's our best compliment," she says.

Owens' Restaurant still uses some of Clara's tried-and-true recipes. They wouldn't think of altering her crab cakes or hush puppies (for those who compare, these are cake-like, no onions). But they recognize that people today want more choices than they did back in 1946. The restaurant serves fried and broiled seafood, but also offers it grilled, steamed, and sautéed. Certified, grain-fed Iowa beef, cut in-house, is one of their specialties. They offer duck, veal, pasta, and entree-sized salads. They're conscious of using seasonal foods, and the menu highlights fresh and regional vegetables from eastern Carolina farms, like game fish straight from Oregon Inlet, and crabs, shrimp, and oysters from the local sounds.

"People's fondest memories are spent over good food and the gathering of family and friends," says Clara Mae. "We try to recreate that experience here every night. We try to make sure it's a warm experience and make people feel special. We treat people like family." — *Molly Harrison*

SAM & OMIE'S

A classic seafood restaurant hooks patrons with its fresh food
and family-style atmosphere.

SAM & OMIE'S
7228 South Virginia Dare Trail, Nags Head, N.C. 27959
phone: (252) 441-7366 *web:* samandomies.net
HOURS: Open daily, 7 a.m.-10 p.m.

JUST AS IT HAS DONE EVERY SEASON SINCE OPENING on June 5, 1937, the Nags Head seafood landmark still draws people off the beach in search of a good meal. The cottage-styled structure hasn't changed over the years — the parking lot is still beach sand, the screen door still squeaks and slams behind you, and a light layer of sand still peppers the hardwood floors inside.

Teresa Merritt and her partner, Carol Sikes, have owned the restaurant since 1987; Merritt started by waiting tables. "Like many of us here, I came, and I stayed," she says. She and Sikes maintain the landmark restaurant to preserve "how it used to be — family and fishing." Back in 1937, Sam & Omie's originated charter boat fishing in Nags Head. "People used to come in, order a meal, then reserve a charter boat to fish offshore," Merritt says, pointing to a small stained glass window near the kitchen that served as the boat charter office before the kitchen was enlarged.

> The landmark restaurant preserves how things used to be: family and fishing.

But tradition isn't confined to the restaurant; it also refers to the people who make it happen — the staff. Merritt says the least-tenured employee, so to speak, is a 10-year veteran. "Our people stay, and our customers like that," she says. Head Chef C.W. Lee stopped by for lunch 25 years ago. After lunch and after mentioning his past kitchen experience in Florida, he was asked to "help out" for the afternoon. He stayed. Lee's specialty is she-crab soup. He makes six gallons a day. Other menu favorites include steamed shrimp, clams, and crab legs; fried oysters and shrimp; marinated tuna and local catches; scratch-made crab cakes; as well as prime rib, fried chicken, homemade desserts, and their famous "Clam Dogs" — a frankfurter roll with fried clam strips and made-from-scratch tartar or cocktail sauce. — *Bryan Oesterreich*

KELLY'S OUTER BANKS RESTAURANT
The upscale eatery combines delectable dishes with engaging entertainment.

KELLY'S
U.S. Highway 158, Milepost 10.5, Nags Head, N.C. 27959
phone: (252) 441-4116 *web:* kellysrestaurant.com

AT KELLY'S, THE EASIEST DECISION IS HOW TO BEGIN: Each table receives a basket of owner Mike Kelly's signature sweet potato biscuits. From here, the choices get more difficult. Among the delectable offerings are Flounder Florentine, a seafood bouillabaisse in a saffron sauce, and cornmeal-fried oysters. For the ultimate sampling of regional flavor, try the North Carolina Seafood Collection, featuring flounder, shrimp, scallops, and crab, all freshly caught from local waters. In the summer, Kelly's keeps things hopping with regional bands as well as some national acts who play in the tavern. — *Elizabeth Hudson*

CAPE
HATTERAS
LIGHTHOUSE

IN THE AREA: BUXTON,
AVON, FRISCO

CHAPTER THREE
CAPE HATTERAS LIGHTHOUSE
TALLEST BRICK TOWER IN THE NATION

ITS BLACK-AND-WHITE SPIRALS EXTENDING NEARLY 200 FEET into the air over Buxton, the Cape Hatteras Lighthouse is one of the most recognized in our nation. After twilight, the sentinel casts a romantic glow over the ocean that can be seen for more than 20 miles.

"That lighthouse totally changed my life," says Kim Mosher, who met her husband at the lighthouse in 1985. "We talk about it sometimes around friends, and Kevin says, 'If I'd never met Kim at that lighthouse, we wouldn't be here today.'"

A photography student at Virginia Commonwealth University, Mosher was on a class trip to the lighthouse when she met the Outer Banks native shortly after he was photographed surfing by another photographer. Today, they live in the shadow of the lighthouse, where Mosher, a full-time artist, incorporates the well-known beacon into colorful paintings of fish and coastal birds. "As I look out my window, there's wildlife, the maritime forest, a bass pond, and beyond that is the park service and the lighthouse. I appreciate everything," she says.

HOW TO GET HERE:
- **Northern entrance:**
Via I-95, take U.S. Highway 64 East toward Rocky Mount. Follow U.S. Highway 64 East through Williamston and Plymouth to the junction with N.C. Highway 12 South.
- **Southern entrance:**
Via the Cedar Island Ferry: From I-40 East, take Exit 306 to U.S. Highway 70 East Follow U.S. Highway 70 East to Sea Level. Take N.C. Highway 12 North to the ferry terminal. The Cedar Island Ferry crosses the Pamlico Sound to Ocracoke Village. Follow N.C. Highway 12 North to the seashore entrance. Ferry crossing time is 2.25 hours; reservations are required.
- **Via the Swan Quarter Ferry**: Take U.S. Highway 264 to N.C. Highway 45 in Swan Quarter. Follow N.C. Highway 45 South to the Hyde County Courthouse. At the courthouse, turn on Oyster Creek Road and follow to the terminal. The Swan Quarter Ferry crosses the Pamlico Sound to Ocracoke Village. Follow N.C. Highway 12 North to the Seashore entrance.

Like Mosher, many people are drawn to the lighthouse, which was built in 1870 from more than 1.2 million bricks. The tallest brick lighthouse in North America, the Cape Hatteras tower continues to stand guard over the Graveyard of the Atlantic. "It marks the most treacherous place along the Outer Banks and one of the most treacherous along the East Coast that mariners faced," says Marcia Lyons, district interpreter at the Cape Hatteras National Seashore. "The specific area that it was warning mariners away from was Diamond Shoals, a series of sand bars that jut out into the ocean."

Beach erosion has threatened the light through the years and led officials to close it in 1936. It was relit in 1950, and in 1999, after heated debate, the lighthouse was moved half a mile from the water's edge. The tower's first-order Fresnel lens was lit on December 18, 1870. Today, the lens — at 12 feet high and six feet in diameter — is a dramatic focal point of the Graveyard of the Atlantic Museum in Hatteras. — *Misti Lee*

MOVING HATTERAS
A MONUMENTAL TASK
WHEN IT WAS BUILT IN 1803, THE LIGHTHOUSE WAS situated a comfortable 1,500 feet from the shoreline. Over the years, the encroaching tide began to claim the distance between the lighthouse and ocean, narrowing it to just 120 feet and setting the lighthouse on the path to certain doom. In 1999, the Hatteras tower was relocated 2,900 feet to the southwest, which should, according to the National Park Service, keep it safe from approaching waves for another 100 years.

LIGHTHOUSE VIEW OCEANFRONT LODGING

Fifty years ago, the Hoopers were the first to welcome guests; today their grandchildren continue to show that family hospitality.

LIGHTHOUSE VIEW OCEANFRONT LODGING
46677 N.C. Highway 12, Buxton, N.C. 27920
phone: (800) 225-7651 *web:* lighthouseview.com

TRY TO IMAGINE WHAT HATTERAS ISLAND was like before the 1950s. That was before the Herbert C. Bonner Bridge was built over the Oregon Inlet, before the Cape Hatteras National Seashore was officially created, and before N.C. Highway 12 was paved down the spine of the island.

After crossing the Oregon Inlet on Toby Tillett's rustic ferry, a car trip down the island was a bumpy ride on a desert-like landscape, fraught with the possibility of getting stuck. You could "ride the wash" alongside the surf if the tide was low or follow the tire-rut tracks in the sand on the "inside road" on the interior of the island.

Along the length of the island, the oceanfront was barren. The locals wouldn't have dreamed of living in the harsh conditions along the ocean, preferring instead to live on the sound side or in protected wooded areas. In the small villages, there wasn't much of a welcome mat laid out for visitors in terms of hotels and restaurants because not too many people visited. Only outdoorsy types, hunters and anglers mostly, found it worth their while to trek down the sandy stretches of the island, where a few accommodations awaited them in Hatteras Village.

In 1947, the state of North Carolina began paving sections of N.C. Highway 12 along the island, and in 1952 the entire path was completed, from Oregon Inlet to Hatteras Inlet. Paved highway access changed Hatteras Island. For the first time, carloads of visitors began lining up at the Oregon

Inlet ferry, waiting their turn to drive down the new, paved road and see what legendary Hatteras Island was all about.

The line at the ferry got even longer after 1953, when the National Park Service officially established the Cape Hatteras National Seashore, the nation's first seashore park, bringing national attention to the wonders of this isolated barrier island.

It was time to start welcoming the tourists.

COTTAGE COURT

The Hooper family was one of the first Hatteras families to serve as host to the new influx of visitors. In 1952, John Edgar Hooper of Buxton built an oceanfront cottage on land given to him by his wife's sister, Maude White. This was the beginning of the Lighthouse View Court motel.

White, who was the postmistress and the unofficial "mayor" of Buxton, had bought a sizeable stretch of oceanfront land for $75. White gave her sister, Annie Miller Hooper, who was married to John Edgar Hooper, and her daughter plots of land on which to build oceanfront motels.

It was time to start welcoming the tourists.

John Edgar and Annie Hooper had spent several years off-island, in Stumpy Point and Norfolk, Virginia, due to the tough nature of making a living on Hatteras. But after World War II, the Hoopers came back to Hatteras, this time settling in Buxton Woods.

The Lighthouse View was on a barren piece of land on the north end of Buxton. The property offered not only ocean views but also, as you might have guessed by the name, great views of the lighthouse, as there was not a single building between the motel and the light.

John Edgar Hooper expanded his motel slowly, adding on one cottage per season. From 1952 to 1963, he built nine cottages. The motel was what's known on the Outer Banks as a "cottage court," a collection of individual cottages with centralized services.

His son, Edgar O. Hooper, who had also moved to Buxton Village after working at Norfolk Naval Shipyard and serving overseas in World War II, ran a general store called Fuller's and Hooper's General Store. But as the motel business grew, Edgar helped out more in his father's business, and Edgar's three children were always there, too.

John Robert remembers that people's beach vacations were different back then. There weren't many choices of places to stay on Hatteras, but still many of the customers rented rooms by walking in off the street. The weekers, those who stayed for a week or longer, communicated with the Hoopers by mail. It was common for families to stay for as long as two or three weeks.

When the Bonner Bridge was completed over Oregon Inlet in 1963, Hatteras Island was in for more dramatic change. No longer impeded by a slow ferry ride, daytrippers and weekenders streamed onto the island. "The island became a giant playground for everyone from Nags Head and beyond," says John Robert.

NEXT GENERATION

After college, John Robert returned to Hatteras Island and worked as a commercial fisherman while his grandfather and father continued to operate the Lighthouse View.

In the mid-1980s, the Hoopers expanded the motel and bought additional acreage along the oceanfront. John Edgar Hooper, who had passed away in the early '80s, never saw the expansion. John Robert helped his father build the new cottages, and that's when the third generation became part of the family business.

John Robert's help was especially needed in 1993, when Hurricane Emily struck Hatteras Island. The sound waters washed completely over the island, and the original motel cottages were destroyed.

Rather than seeing it as a setback, Edgar and John Robert saw it as an opportunity to modernize and upgrade their facilities to compete with the increasing number of motels on the island. Now known as Lighthouse View Oceanfront Lodging, today there are 85 units, ranging from motel rooms to one-bedroom villas to four-bedroom cottages.

Besides the new buildings, the character of the Lighthouse View is much the same today as it was when John Edgar Hooper first opened the motel. The Hooper family hospitality has been drawing some customers back for more than 50 years. John Robert still sees some of the kids he played with when he was young, now returning with their children for a week at the beach. "This business has been good to the Hooper family," says John Robert. And the Hoopers have made sure it also has been good to the vacationers of Hatteras Island. — *Molly Harrison*

FRISCO NATIVE AMERICAN MUSEUM

A lifetime of collecting authentic Indian artifacts is the foundation for a special museum in Frisco.

FRISCO NATIVE AMERICAN MUSEUM
N.C. Highway 12, Frisco, N.C. 27936
phone: (252) 995-4440 *web:* nativeamericanmuseum.org

HOURS: Tuesday-Sunday, 11 a.m.-5 p.m.
Winter Hours Adjusted.
ADMISSION: $5 per person, $15 per family, $3 for seniors.

FOOT FOR FOOT AND POUND FOR POUND, you probably won't see as many Native American artifacts in one place anywhere else in the state. Some of the hundreds of thousands of American Indian artifacts packed into this small museum are associated with North Carolina Indians, but the vast bulk comes from Indian peoples across America and far back into history. You'll see ancient PaleoIndian spear points and Archaic arrowheads. Baskets are everywhere, from the Cherokee, Apache, and scores of other peoples. You'll see Mohawk beadwork, Hopi drums, Plains Indian headdresses and coup sticks, a Pueblo pictograph, the remnant of a centuries-old Outer Banks dugout canoe, as well as pottery, cradleboards, moccasins, snowshoes, rattles, and clothing from just about every Indian nation you can imagine.

And this just scratches the surface. The Frisco Native American Museum is a private, homegrown museum. It'll cost you five bucks to tour, and after you go through it, you'll likely meet the owners, Carl and Joyce Bornfriend.

A LOVE FOR COLLECTING

Carl, who grew up in Philadelphia, developed a bent for collecting. He was interested in Native American artifacts and art. "I began collecting as a nine-year-old boy," he says. "I wanted something that was authentically American.

So I began trading military medals and weapons for Native American stuff."
As his collection grew, his efforts to preserve Native American relics earned
him high marks with Native American people, and he was adopted by the
Lenni Lenape Indians of Pennsylvania.

In the early 1980s, he moved to the Outer Banks, bringing with him his
100,000-plus-item Indian artifact collection. He taught school and met his
wife, Joyce, a native Outer Banker who also has tremendous respect for
American Indian culture and art. Together, they decided to exhibit Carl's ever-
growing artifact collection.

By the late 1980s, the couple acquired the gift shop next to their home,
and the Frisco Native American Museum was born. Even then it was a tight
squeeze — there were so many artifacts that had to be packed into the small
building. The aisles are cramped, as virtually every available space in the
museum bulges with displays of artifacts, maps, and other items.

More than just a storehouse of artifacts, the Bornfriends see their collection
as a teaching museum. It shows the
genius of Native Americans and
explains their remarkable history. The
couple encourages school tours and
often arranges specific class or topic
requests. Carl and Joyce believe in

> Virtually every available space bulges with displays of artifacts, maps, and other items.

hands-on history, so their programs provide more than a lecture. Students
get to handle artifacts, and Carl normally gives one to each student. "I want
them to have a real Native American artifact," Carl says. "And I won't put out
anything that's not authentic."

The Bornfriends's enthusiasm for the museum is spreading. Visitors from
across the state and as far away as Germany and Indonesia have toured. It's
listed in the Historic Albemarle Tour Heritage Trail brochure. Scholars of
Native American history and anthropology have done research here. *National
Geographic* came down once to take pictures. Native Americans often visit,
signing the guestbook with such tribal identities as Cheyenne, Cherokee,
Seminole, Alabama-Coushatta, and Oglala Sioux. — *David La Vere*

EXPLORE

GRAVEYARD OF THE ATLANTIC MUSEUM

On the Outer Banks, a museum is as treasured
as the artifacts it houses.

GRAVEYARD OF THE ATLANTIC MUSEUM
59200 Museum Drive, Hatteras, N.C. 27943
phone: (252) 986-2995 *web:* graveyardoftheatlantic.com

HOURS: Monday-Friday, 10 a.m.-4 p.m. **ADMISSION:** Free; donations appreciated.

OVER THE COURSE OF FOUR CENTURIES, seafaring vessels have traversed the tempestuous ocean waters that have been known, nearly as long, as the Graveyard of the Atlantic. The first ships came for exploration and discovery. Later, most participated in commerce, some took part in piracy, still others were engaged in warfare. In all, more than 1,000 unlucky vessels, their crews, and passengers were forced to make the ocean waters and beaches along North Carolina's Outer Banks their final port of call.

A staggering collection of historic artifacts — Roman coins and pirate doubloons, anchors, signal lamps, ship's bells, name boards, captain's desks, mysterious portraits, cannonballs, torpedoes, sextants, wine bottles, taffrail logs, portholes, and even top-secret military code machines — has spilled onto the beaches. And every treasure of the Graveyard of the Atlantic has an astonishing tale to tell.

LET'S MAKE A DEAL

"Are you the owner of that small dinghy there?" asked the stranger as he held an odd-looking spear and a pair of Japanese pearl-diver goggles.

It was a calm day on the beach at Kill Devil Hills during the summer of 1938. The spearfisherman, a Marine major stationed at Quantico, Virginia, addressed a young entrepreneur. After the 18-year-old confirmed that the dinghy was his, the athletic-looking major asked if the lad could row him out to the wrecks just north of the Croatan Inn. The Marine was interested in spearing sheepshead, a hard-to-hook but delicious fish known to congregate around bridge pilings and shipwrecks. The two men made a deal.

Through gentle breakers, the youth deftly rowed a quarter-mile to the remains of the two vessels that foundered in storms in 1927 and 1929. There, the spearfisherman grabbed his gear, took a deep breath, and disappeared over the stern of the little boat. Before too long, the major reappeared with an enormous sheepshead. He then offered the young man a chance to do the same, and Outer Banks history was forever changed.

100,000 copies and more than a half-century later, his book is still in print.

The teen slipped over the side of his seven-foot skiff and soon discovered a ghostly world unknown to most — legendary underwater shipwrecks and their untold tales of travail, tragedy, and treasure. It was on that day that David Stick, the young, aspiring writer and dinghy owner, was captivated by the Graveyard of the Atlantic and the mysteries of North Carolina's maritime heritage. Fourteen years later, after "goggle-fishing" the wrecks of the steamers *Kyzikes* and *Carl Gerhard*, hitchhiking across America, and serving as a WWII war correspondent, Stick finally sat down and wrote *The Graveyard of the Atlantic: Shipwrecks of the North Carolina Coast*. One hundred thousand copies and more than a half-century later, his book is still in print. The book has done more than sell — it has launched tens of thousands of vacations to the North Carolina coast, and many of its fans have moved to the Outer Banks to be immersed in its legacy.

WORTH THE TIME

There was a time when shipwrecks were big business on the Outer Banks and provided jobs in the lighthouse service, the lifesaving service, and the salvage industry. In the early 19th century, at the behest of shipping companies and their insurance underwriters, government got involved, establishing wreck districts and appointing wreck commissioners or vendue (auction) Masters to secure disabled vessels and their cargo for resale.

Many of the rare and valuable artifacts that have survived throughout the ages were bid for and purchased by islanders at auctions, usually at the very scene of the wreck. Practical items were put to immediate use — unspoiled food, spirits, cooking utensils, china, furniture, lamps, books, clothing, cordage, rigging, tackle, and lifeboats. Many other treasures have left the state, potentially forever.

In the 1970s, when the U.S.S. *Monitor* was finally discovered after resting on the ocean floor off Hatteras Inlet for 110 years, U.S. Navy archeologists sought a museum to store, conserve, and display artifacts from the warship. No suitable facility existed on the Outer Banks, and eventually the Mariner's Museum of Newport News was chosen to house the ironclad's remains.

Business and political leaders from Dare and Hyde counties recognized the need for a museum dedicated to the unique history and legacy of the Outer Banks, rescued from obscurity by David Stick more than 34 years earlier. In 1988 and 1992, Congress authorized the Secretary of Commerce, through the National Oceanographic and Atmospheric Administration, to establish a public, nonprofit, educational institution dedicated to the preservation and interpretation of shipwreck artifacts from the Graveyard of the Atlantic.

> Leaders recognized the need for a museum dedicated to the history of the Outer Banks.

PRICELESS ARTIFACTS

Located adjacent to the Hatteras-Ocracoke ferry docks in Hatteras Village, the Graveyard of the Atlantic Museum building is worthy of the daunting and time-consuming effort required of its founders.

The architecture and massive, curved beams of the structure evoke the spirit of seafaring vessels. The 19,000-square-foot climate-controlled facility, housed under a seven-layer, impermeable roof, was designed to withstand sustained winds of more than 135 miles per hour. At 12 feet above sea level, it also surpasses the 1,000-year flood plain and may be used as a shelter of last resort during storms. The museum's fortress-like engineering and construction were funded for a simple reason: to safely harbor four centuries of priceless historic artifacts.

These artifacts — like the centerpiece exhibit Fresnel lens from the Hatteras Lighthouse — are the pillars of our lost past, evidence that a bygone world, known only through the words of historians, existed. Even more stunning is that many of these treasures landed on the Outer Banks from half a world away more than 2,000 years ago. — *Kevin Duffus*

SEA STORIES

Few things go together better than the beach
and a good book.

BUXTON VILLAGE BOOKS
47918 N.C. Highway 12, Buxton, N.C. 27920
phone: (252) 995-4240 *web:* buxtonvillagebooks.com

BUXTON VILLAGE BOOKS OCCUPIES A FRIENDLY COTTAGE
with a creaky floor in the heart of a town best known for the Cape
Hatteras Lighthouse. The building had been a vintage island cottage when
Gee Gee Rosell converted it to a bookshop in 1984. Before that, in the
early 1900s, it was a general store. In the course of restoration, Rosell made
a wonderful discovery. "When I stripped the walls down to the original
construction," she says, "I found they'd been built of ship's timbers."

The shop offers a wide selection of sea stories, Southern fiction, saltwater
fly-fishing books, and books on Outer Banks history. Cookbooks are a
specialty here, and the shop has been a great island gathering spot.

"A bookshop is all about intellectual curiosity," says Rosell. "So, it's
really been a local gathering place on a daily basis from the outset." She
has met many authors and made many friends. "People come back year after
year. I may not always know their names, but I know about their pets and
kids." — *Charles Blackburn Jr.*

FOR FISHING FANATICS

Golden sun, a pounding surf, and a fish on the end of your line.
Sounds like paradise.

AVON FISHING PIER
41001 N.C. Highway 12, Avon, N.C. 27915
phone: (252) 995-5480 *web:* avonpier.com

FRANK AND FRAN'S FISHERMAN'S FRIEND
40210 N.C. Highway 12, Avon, N.C. 27915
phone: (252) 995-4171 *web:* hatteras-island.com

FISHERMEN AND WOMEN ANGLING for a good time will want to cast a line at the newly renovated, 600-foot Avon Fishing Pier, renowned as one of the best places in the world to catch red drum. In fact, in 1984, a world-record drum — 94 pounds, 2 ounces — was snagged here. An annual red drum tournament, held each fall when the drum make their migration past Hatteras Island, promises plenty of friendly competition and more than a few fish tales. And, along with the surf, this pier also has turf: an 18-hole all-grass putting green on the premises.

On your way to the pier, stop in at Frank and Fran's, a family-owned tackle shop and official weigh station in Avon, for a complimentary cup of coffee, ice for your cooler, and a few supplies for the fish, as well. Frank and Fran's stocks plenty of bait and tackle, as well as a good selection of cigars, to help pass the time on those days when the fish just aren't biting. — *Elizabeth Hudson*

ISLAND EATS

For spots that others might not notice, take a table
at one of these Hatteras establishments.

THE CAPTAIN'S TABLE
47048 N.C. Highway 12, Buxton, N.C. 27920
phone: (252) 995-3117

POP'S RAW BAR AND RESTAURANT
48967 N.C. Highway 12, Buxton, N.C. 27920
phone: (252) 995-7734

BONNIE ROWE'S BROTHER IS A COMMERCIAL FISHERMAN, someone who pulls from local waters and sells to local restaurants. So Bonnie, owner of Vacation Traditions in Rodanthe, doesn't take the phrase "local seafood" lightly. Trust her, then, when it comes to fresh food on Hatteras Island.

The Captain's Table in Buxton, Rowe says, is a local place with a passion. Ricky Scarborough, who owns the restaurant with his wife, Donna, is a commercial fisherman himself. Often, he's on the water in the morning, and at the restaurant in the evening. The portions are generous and fresh as can be.

Most people pass Pop's Raw Bar and Restaurant without blinking. Don't. It specializes in steamed seafood — local, of course. While you have your hands deep in piles of shrimp, clams, oysters, or crab legs, you might find a few local folks tossing darts over a beer. Rowe met her husband, Woody, here.

"It's a quirky little place that has really good food," Rowe says. "A lot of people probably pass it by, because it's a dive. But that's what we seek out when we go places." — *Michael Graff*

NORTH CAROLINA
LIGHTHOUSES

Enduring symbols of our state, these landmarks
have defined our coastline for generations,
guiding us, protecting us, and inspiring us.

CAPE HATTERAS
LIGHTHOUSE
Photograph by Ray Matthews

OCRACOKE LIGHTHOUSE
Photograph by Ray Matthews

BALD HEAD ISLAND LIGHTHOUSE
Photograph by Scott Taylor

CAPE LOOKOUT LIGHTHOUSE
Photograph by Ray Matthews

OAK ISLAND LIGHTHOUSE
Photograph by Scott Taylor

BODIE ISLAND LIGHTHOUSE
Photograph by Ray Matthews

CURRITUCK BEACH LIGHTHOUSE
Photograph by Ray Matthews

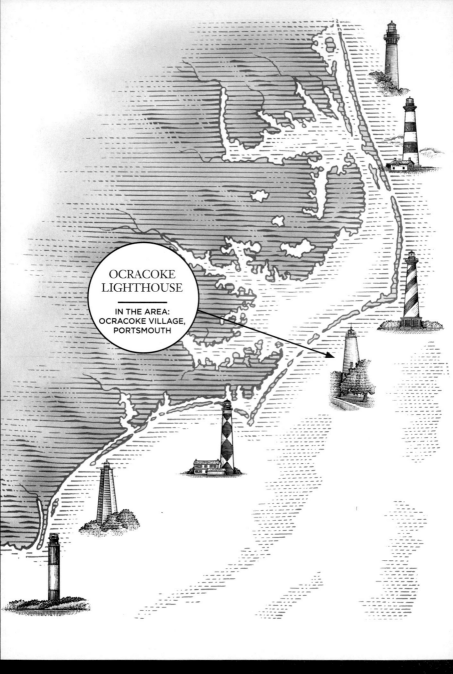

OCRACOKE
LIGHTHOUSE

IN THE AREA:
OCRACOKE VILLAGE,
PORTSMOUTH

CHAPTER FOUR

OCRACOKE LIGHTHOUSE
OLDEST OPERATIONAL LIGHT

AWHITE, STUCCO-COVERED TOWER is one of the first sights to greet visitors coming into the harbor on Ocracoke Island by ferry. The Ocracoke Lighthouse, punctuating the end of a white picket fence in Ocracoke Village, is a sweet welcome sign to visitors and residents alike.

Built in 1823, the Ocracoke tower is the oldest working lighthouse in the state. At about 75 feet tall, according to the National Park Service, it's shorter than North Carolina's other lights. "It was never intended to be a light beacon for ships that were far offshore," according to Marcia Lyons, district interpreter at the Cape Hatteras National Seashore. "It was mostly a light that was there to tell mariners where the inlet was, where the harbor was."

Ocracoke native Rudy Austin was born and raised in his grandmother's house a few hundred feet from the lighthouse, a fixture of his childhood. "It was really our only streetlight when we were growing up," he says, laughing.

His mother and grandmother often told him the story of how they rode out

HOW TO GET HERE:

- Take N.C. Highway 12 south from Buxton, allow 30 minutes driving time in the summer to reach the Ocracoke ferry at the southern tip of Hatteras Island.

- Check the state-run (no charge) car/passenger ferry schedules on **outer-banks.com/ferry** and get an idea when you can cross between Hatteras and Ocracoke islands. The ferry ride is 45 minutes across Pamlico Sound to the ferry dock at the north end of Ocracoke Island. Drive 12 miles south on the continuation of N.C. Highway 12 into the village of Ocracoke.

the hurricane of 1944, when he was 2 years old, on the second story of their house, while others sought shelter inside the light keeper's house. Family friend Andy Anderson, who was in the United States Coast Guard, helped rescue people in the midst of the storm. With Anderson's help, about 25 people escaped the rising waters inside the lighthouse keeper's quarters.

After the floodwaters receded, villagers found their clothing washed from their homes and left hanging on the picket fence by the lighthouse, as if it had been hung out to dry.

When he's out in his boat or on the ferry coming to Ocracoke, Austin still gets a peaceful feeling of home when the light begins to shine over the island. "I wouldn't live anywhere that didn't have a ferry boat, a lighthouse, and an air strip," he says. — *Misti Lee*

For a ride through the Ocracoke Inlet with Rudy Austin and his boat, see our story on page 63.

A LITTLE LIGHT CLEANING:
HOW OCRACOKE STAYED GLEAMING

MIX UNSLAKED LIME WITH BOILING WATER, SALT, POWDERED SPANISH WHITING, AND GROUND RICE. Stir in more boiling water and clear glue, and mix until smooth. Apply while hot. A down-home cure for poison ivy? Nope — it's the original "whitewash" recipe that was recommended by the United States Lighthouse Board (now the Lighthouse Service) for keeping the Ocracoke Lighthouse's exterior at its gleaming finest. See the results firsthand at the oldest operating lighthouse in the nation.

STAY AND SLEEP

THURSTON HOUSE INN
Enjoy an Ocracoke stay in a home with a close connection to the sea.

THURSTON HOUSE INN
671 N.C. Highway 12, Ocracoke, N.C. 27960
phone: (252) 928-6037 *web:* thurstonhouseinn.com

TONY THURSTON GASKILL WAS A TRUE Ocracoke Islander. The Gaskill family heritage on Ocracoke dates back to the 1700s, and he was born on the island in 1902. His family owned the Pamlico Inn on Ocracoke from the 1920s through the 1940s. During World War II, Gaskill captained the *Nettie B*, a Navy supply boat that ran from Ocracoke to Cherry Point. Later, with his own boat, *Southwind*, Captain Thurston became a well-known guide for fishing and hunting parties. But when Gaskill wasn't off on an adventure, he spent much of his time at the home he built in Ocracoke in 1925.

The spacious, 2,000-square-foot house remained his private residence until Gaskill and his wife, Nora, entered a nursing home in 1995. In 1996, Gaskill's granddaughter, Marlene, and her husband, Randal Mathews, renovated and converted the family home into a bed and breakfast. In 2005, the Mathewses sold the bed and breakfast to another member of Captain Thurston's family. Donna Boor, Marlene's sister, purchased the inn and enlisted her mother, Annie Louise Gaskill Gaskins, Captain Thurston's daughter, who grew up in the house.

Today, Boor and Gaskins greet their guests in the morning with coffee, tea, or juice, as well as fresh fruit, assorted danishes, cereals, and their most popular breakfast entrée, sweet potato pancakes. They also serve an island favorite: Ocracoke fig cake.

Since the Thurston House Inn has been in the women's family for 84 years, they feel at home here, and they happily extend the experience to all their guests.

— L.A. Jackson

STAY AND SLEEP

OCRACOKE HARBOR INN

Seclusion and a view of Silver Lake Harbor beckon Ocracoke guests.

OCRACOKE HARBOR INN
144 Silver Lake Road, Ocracoke, N.C. 27960
phone: (888) 456-1998 *web:* ocracokeharborinn.com

OCRACOKE ISLAND IS CUT OFF from the rest of North Carolina, and for those looking for solitude and relaxation, it can be said that it is also cut off from the rest of the world. No bridges connect Ocracoke to the mainland, so ferry, private boat, or private airplane are the only ways to reach this thin slice of land between the vast Pamlico Sound and the Atlantic Ocean.

In the early 1960s, on the south end of the town's Silver Lake Harbor, many travelers frequented Lakeside Cottages. In 1997, the property was sold, and the buildings were moved to make way for the Ocracoke Harbor Inn, which opened in May 1998.

Today, the 11,000-square-foot inn provides comfort and relaxation for guests looking to slow down their busy lives, if only for a few days. The inn is accommodating no matter how guests get to Ocracoke. Typical travelers take the auto ferry, and parking spaces are available for cars. Guests flying in with private planes, however, can be picked up by the inn's staff at the small airstrip south of town. In addition, with advance reservation, private boat owners can dock beside the inn.

There are 16 rooms and seven suites, each with a private deck to enjoy the maritime magic that surrounds the inn. All the units have coffeemakers and refrigerators and come with either two queen-size beds or one king-size. The suites, most of which are on the third floor, include separate bedrooms, kitchenettes, Jacuzzi tubs, and great views.

In the morning, guests enjoy a continental breakfast on the inn's waterfront deck, the ideal spot from which to watch the fishing boats depart for a day at sea. Afteward, guests who want to spend a day exploring Ocracoke village may rent a bicycle for the adventure or simply walk, because the inn's central location is convenient to all the sights and activities in town. — *L.A. Jackson*

EXPLORE

ISLAND MUSIC:
DEEPWATER THEATER AND MUSIC HALL

Members of Molasses Creek settle into the rhythms of their beloved Ocracoke and invite visitors to sing along.

MOLASSES CREEK
25 School Road, Ocracoke, N.C. 27960
phone: (252) 928-3411 *web:* molassescreek.com

GRAVEL CRUNCHES BENEATH OUR FEET as we walk from the car toward the Ocracoke Community Center. The parking lot is full — mostly pickup trucks with salt spray on their flanks, surf-casting rods on their front bumpers, and license tags that read OBX. A Day-Glo orange poster stapled to a wooden stake out by the road announces "Tonight! The Ocrafolk Opry!"

Along the back wall of the one-story, wood-sided building, a counter displays home-baked goods for sale. A line of folding chairs, filled with people of all ages dressed in casual clothes, faces the modest stage. Two bleached-blonde toddlers chase each other up and down the center aisle. The lights dim as a voice announces: "Good evening. Please welcome — Molasses Creek!" Sunburned hands come together as Gary Mitchell and "Fiddler Dave" raise their instruments and island magic ensues.

This island — barely 16 miles long — has a legacy of commercial fishing, community (permanent residents number fewer than 1,000), and a true "island spirit." Here, where storms come ashore, people come together. They also come together to celebrate their lives in song. The members of Molasses Creek decided they wanted to be a part of preserving the music and culture of the Outer Banks and Ocracoke.

Mitchell and his wife, Kitty, had been playing together since the mid-1970s when they came across Fiddler Dave Tweedie in 1993. Tweedie was taking classes at Davidson College in Davidson when the duo convinced him to join them and move to Ocracoke. Tweedie, a native of Oklahoma, says all it took was a weekend on the island. "How can anyone not fall in love with Ocracoke?" he says. The fiddle he plays was his grandmother's. "I think of her every time I perform — she's always with me."

Mitchell plays acoustic guitar. Before crafting melodies, he worked as a carpenter building homes. He says those long days and hard work prepared him for the work it takes to be a successful musician. Kitty, who played bass with the band for several years, retired from the group to focus on her painting — for years, she taught art, music, and Spanish at Ocracoke School — and Lou Castro, his wife, Marcy, and Gerald Hampton joined the group, stepping in a few years ago as if they'd been part of this band forever. Nine albums so far attest to the group's chemistry and talent.

On Ocracoke, they've created a venue where residents can enjoy not only the Creek's performances, but local talent as well. The Deepwater Theater sits among lazy live oaks on School Road. The intimate theater seats 100 and gives island residents and visitors the opportunity to hear music "in a theater environment as opposed to a club atmosphere where distractions detract from the experience," says Mitchell.

Molasses Creek also fosters the feeling of community at home on the island. Ocracoke native Elizabeth Chamberlin, who with her husband, Captain George, provides visitors with accommodations at their Captain's Landing Hotel, sings the praises of the group. "Our guests are always happy to hear a performance at the Deepwater Theater is scheduled when they visit," says Chamberlin, who is proud of her island's cultural heritage. "When Molasses Creek began playing here, they were inspired by Ocracoke — now Ocracoke is inspired by Molasses Creek." — *Bryan A. Oesterreich*

SIGHTSEEING PORTSMOUTH

Hop over to Portsmouth Village for a glimpse into Outer Banks history.

AUSTIN BOAT TOURS
Daily boat tours from Ocracoke Harbor
phone: (252) 928-4361 *web:* portsmouthnc.com

CAPTAIN RUDY AUSTIN HAS BEEN NAVIGATING the silty shoals of Ocracoke Inlet since the 1970s, when he would accompany his father, who transported sportsmen to a hunting and fishing lodge that was on Portsmouth Island at the time. Now, he ferries several hundred visitors a year to Portsmouth, telling stories in his native "hoi toide" brogue about the pirate vessels and German U-boats that haunted these waters in the past.

On Portsmouth, Captain Austin drops you at the Haulover Point Dock, where you'll walk up to the village, feet sinking into the soft sand of the path. Apart from the handful of day-trippers, the village seems deserted. Some call it a ghost town, but look closer. You'll notice that one house has a bright coat of yellow paint; another, a new shingle roof, the unweathered wood still yellow. Sawhorses and lumber sit out in front of another house. Things are going on in Portsmouth. It may be frozen in time, but it hasn't been ruined by it.

> It may be frozen in time, but it hasn't been ruined by it.

More than 20 buildings remain on the site of what was once one of the Outer Banks' largest towns and busiest seaports. Chartered in 1753, Portsmouth rose to prominence as a lightering station. The lightering trade was necessary for supplying North Carolina's inland ports, such as Edenton, Bath, and New Bern. Oceangoing ships had to transfer their cargo to smaller, shallow-draught boats that could navigate the sounds. During the late 18th and early 19th centuries, Ocracoke Inlet was the most important gateway to the Atlantic between Norfolk, Virginia, and Wilmington. In 1842, a powerful hurricane opened Hatteras and Oregon inlets. Ocracoke's and Portsmouth's busy maritime commerce quickly evaporated, and the two towns evolved into fishing villages.

Portsmouth remained a small, vibrant community, but throughout the 20th century, the island's population declined. There were other misfortunes, too. A pair of hurricanes drove many off the island in 1933, and the U.S. Coast Guard shut down the lifesaving station in 1937. The menhaden fish processing plant on nearby Casey Island burned, and the Portsmouth school and post office closed. In 1971, the last two permanent residents, Elma Dixon and Marion Babb, left the island.

PORTSMOUTH TODAY

The main steward for Portsmouth Village today is the federal government. The National Park Service took custody of the land in 1976 and has been committed ever since to maintaining the existing buildings on Portsmouth.

The Henry Piggott house, for example, is a neat, gabled cottage with a charmingly off-center front door. The house's namesake was the town's longtime postmaster and last male resident. Piggott was the descendant of slaves who transferred cargo from the oceangoing ships back in Portsmouth's lightering days. In the 1950s, Piggott was interviewed by a New York reporter who thought he was crazy to be living without electricity on a virtually deserted island. "I've been to New York," Piggott replied, "and I'm not sure which of us is crazy."

Visitors can get a bird's-eye view of the island from atop the old lifesaving station built by the U.S. Coast Guard in the 1890s. Those who are not afraid of heights can climb the ladder to the small lookout on the top floor and see that the village seems to amble out toward the Pamlico Sound. The neat Craftsman cottages planted on the marshes remain a testament to the diligence of the villagers who worked to build a respectable community in such an inhospitable clime. Portsmouth's beauty can be seen not just in its isolation but in the way the individual properties are tied to one another by footpaths and small bridges.

After visitors have eaten their picnic lunches and searched for seashells on the beach, Captain Austin picks them up at the Wallace Channel Dock. Asked how long he intends to provide passage between Ocracoke and Portsmouth, he replies, "As long as people keep coming." — *Glenn Perkins*

OCRACOKE GHOST WALK

Ocracoke Island's Howard Street sets a perfectly eerie stage for the ghost stories that haunt our state's coast.

OCRACOKE GHOST WALK AND HISTORIC TOUR
Tuesday and Friday nights, late spring through fall, except October 31
phone: (252) 928-6300 *web:* villagecraftsmen.com/historywalk.htm

BLACKBEARD SEARCHES FOR HIS HEAD. Shipwreck victims haunt beachgoers. Vaporous images hover in Springer's Point. Unsettled ghosts roam. Long-sunk ships still pass in the night. Ocracoke Island — with its dark lanes, gnarled live oaks, old homes, and abundant cemeteries — offers a perfect backdrop for haunting tales. Eighth-generation Ocracoker Philip Howard details each story on the Ocracoke Ghost Walk and Historic Tour.

The walking tours — there are two from which to chose and each one is a mile-and-a-half long — start on secluded Howard Street and include a brief introductory history of the island followed by 90 minutes of rousing ghost stories, legends, and lore that have been handed down across the generations.

> "People who visit here are interested in more than just getting suntans."

Howard lets the stories speak for themselves; the guides don't dress up or try to intentionally spook anyone. Howard says he's never seen a ghost. "I want people to know that this is a real community with real people who have collected stories over generations," says Howard. "People who visit here are interested in more than just getting suntans. They want to feel a connection to the community." — *Molly Harrison*

OCRACOKE'S FAMOUS FIGS

Plentiful and succulent, the golden fruit provides a tasty link
to the island's past.

BACK PORCH RESTAURANT AND WINE BAR
110 Back Road, Ocracoke, N.C. 27960
phone: (252) 928-6401

---

*Along with the Back Porch Restaurant, there are several more venues, mentioned below,
in which to sample local figs on Ocracoke.*

SEEMINGLY EVERY OTHER YARD ON OCRACOKE ISLAND has a fig tree, often as tall as the house, its palm-sized leaves branching out in wild directions and a mound of oyster and clam shells purposefully piled around its base. The island's sandy soil and salty conditions make it the perfect host to the fruit tree, which is native to the Mediterranean. It's documented that local residents have been growing figs on the island since at least the late 1700s.

> **"Tasting the local figs is essential to the Ocracoke experience."**

Fig cakes are a hot item on Ocracoke Island. They're always on the table at bake sales, picnics, bazaars, and funerals, and vacationers order them to take home because they travel well. Order a fig cake from Della Gaskill at her shop, Woccocon Nursery and Gifts, or from Gaynelle Tillett at the Fish House, or find it on the menu at local restaurants such as The Fig Tree Bakery or The Back Porch Restaurant, which serves an updated fig cake with cream cheese icing.

You'll also find many opportunities to taste fig preserves on the island: Carol Ritchie serves her own preserves at the Beach House Bed and Breakfast, and she pours extra fig syrup over banana pancakes. Erin O'Neal serves her preserves at The Cove Bed and Breakfast. You can find them for sale at stores all over the island — the Ocracoke Preservation Museum, Village Craftsmen, the Fish House, Woccocon Nursery and Gifts, the Variety Store. Local restaurateurs also get creative with figs. Susie O'Neal at the Flying Melon Cafe serves a fig tart, a cream-cheese base topped with sliced figs and a fig preserve glaze, and Ruth Toth at Cafe Atlantic serves a rosemary chevre and fig preserve crostini. No matter what form they're in, fresh or cooked, tasting the local figs is essential to the Ocracoke experience. — *Molly Harrison*

HOWARD'S PUB AND RAW BAR

Mouthwatering mussels and shellfish are only part of the appeal at the popular restaurant, where people come from all over to get in on the fun.

HOWARD'S PUB AND RAW BAR
1175 Irvin Garrish Highway, Ocracoke, N.C. 27960
phone: (252) 928-4441 *web:* howardspub.com

IT WAS ALWAYS ME and my ink-stained friends from my college newspaper who came for the ring toss and the oysters. We'd hang near the door, have a few beers, and swing the quarter-sized ring toward the hook until summer shadows stretched across the wood-slat floor. For us, time stood still. Since then, we've grown up, grown older, had kids. Still, every summer, we come to Ocracoke to sit amid the wallpaper of college pennants and license plates, catch up, eat our steamed oysters, and throw our ring. We come to get away. We want to imbibe within easy reach of the legend of Blackbeard and let our worries dissipate like barroom smoke in our rearview mirror. And that's what happens at Howard's. You come to an island no more than a half-mile wide and arrive by ferry. Then, after driving for at least 13 miles beside the Atlantic on the island's only road, you see the big sign from at least a half-mile away. The first stop on the right. Howard's Pub. — *Jeri Rowe*

CAPE
LOOKOUT
LIGHTHOUSE

IN THE AREA:
BEAUFORT,
MOREHEAD CITY

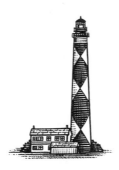

CHAPTER FIVE

CAPE LOOKOUT LIGHTHOUSE

DIAMOND IN THE ROUGH

CONSTRUCTED IN 1859, CAPE LOOKOUT was the first tall lighthouse to be built along North Carolina's coast and remains the only lighthouse in the country with the black-and-white checkers pattern on its tower.

Located on Core Banks Island and overlooking a 10-mile stretch of dangerous waters called Lookout Shoals, it can be reached by boat or passenger ferry from Beaufort and Harkers Island. At 165 feet tall, the lighthouse emits one white flash every 15 seconds, a signal that can be seen 19 nautical miles out to sea.

The "diagonal checkers" daymark gives the lighthouse a distinctive look. "They wanted to have three different patterns on the lighthouses to make them look different — diagonal checkers, the barber pole stripes that are on Hatteras, and the horizontal bands that are on Bodie Island," says Karen Duggan, a ranger with the Cape Lookout National Seashore. "The idea was to have them repeating up and down the coast. That idea came true to a point,

HOW TO GET HERE:
Only one section of Cape Lookout National Seashore is reachable by car — the Visitor Center located on the eastern end of Harkers Island, approximately 20 miles east of Beaufort and 30 miles south of the Cedar Island terminus of the North Carolina State Ferry route from Ocracoke Island to Cedar Island.

- **From Beaufort:** Take U.S. Highway 70 east to Harkers Island Road. From Cedar Island: Take SR 12 south past the Atlantic turnoff to U.S. Highway 70 west. Continue on U.S. Highway 70 to Harkers Island Road, until it dead-ends. The Visitor Center is on the left.
- **By private ferry:** Several styles and sizes of boats are used as ferries. Passengers are delivered directly onto the sound-side beach. Larger ferries, some carrying up to 80 passengers, make use of the docks. The National Park Service provides a list of private ferry operators, leaving from South Core Banks and Shackleford Banks, at **nps.gov/calo/planyourvisit/ferry.htm**

but Cape Lookout Lighthouse is the only one that ended up with a diagonal checkers pattern."

Although some humorous stories suggest the painters mixed up the patterns, the lighthouse was intended to receive the black-and-white "diagonal checkers." As it turns out, the painters did an exceptional job, painting the tower so perfectly it can almost be used as a compass. When standing in front of the lighthouse, if you see dark squares, you're looking north or south, Duggan says. If you see white squares, you're looking east or west. "It's just by the nature of how they laid it out that you can do that — just by lucky chance," Duggan says. "You can walk people around the lighthouse, and it changes. If you walk one way, it looks like it's a black lighthouse with white diamonds. If you walk another way, you've got a white lighthouse with black diamonds." — *Misti Lee*

THE ISLAND EXPERIENCE
CAPE LOOKOUT CABINS

ON THE SOUTH CORE BANKS, 21 rustic cabins rise from the sea grass and sand at Cape Lookout National Seashore, creating an ideal beach getaway. The cabins are wired for generator use, but visitors must bring their own generators. Each cabin has a hot water heater, table, chairs, and a kitchen with cabinets, a propane oven/stove combination, and a private bath. To reserve a cabin, call (252) 728-0942.

STAY AND SLEEP

OUTER BANKS HOUSEBOATS

Oceanfront historic cottages enable guests to live like
a lighthouse keeper.

OUTER BANKS HOUSEBOATS
324 Front Street, Beaufort, N.C. 28516
phone: (252) 728-4129 *web:* outerbankshouseboats.com

ONE OF THE MANY BEAUTIES of the Crystal Coast area of North Carolina is the amount of unspoiled coastline awaiting exploration. Those in the know don't have to come back to civilization as the sun sets; if you've rented a houseboat for the weekend, you're already "home" for the night.

Perry Barrow, Outer Banks Houseboats owner, who has owned and operated Outer Banks Ferry Service for more than 15 years, started offering houseboat rentals in 2003. "Quite simply, my ferry customers were looking for a way to stay out at Cape Lookout, rather than having to take the ferry back at the end of the day," he says.

Outer Banks Houseboats will deliver, anchor, and pick up the houseboat. You need only unpack once, and you'll have ample opportunities for independent exploration (each houseboat rental comes with a 21-foot Carolina Skiff). When everyone else has to head back to land, you can eat in or, if you prefer, head to an area restaurant before spending the night on the water.

TAKE IT EASY

You don't have to drive the boat to enjoy it. Barrow or another captain typically pilot the houseboat to the anchorage of choice — a factor that depends on the wind and waves, as well as desired pursuits once anchored. One or more of the houseboat renters then follow in the Carolina Skiff, providing the perfect opportunity to practice piloting the easy-to-operate skiff and also a general "map" of how to get back to Beaufort in the skiff, if desired. Some renters choose to leave the houseboat at Barrow's dock for one or more

> ## Your houseboat serves as a haven and base for exploring Cape Lookout National Seashore.

of their rental nights to better enjoy a special event or Beaufort nightlife. Most, however, head out to quieter anchorages.

Guests staying more than two nights will get a short visit from Barrow or one of his staff to check on gas, propane, and holding tanks (renters only pay for the gas, oil, and propane they use on the houseboat and skiff).

Once out on Cape Lookout proper, it's just a matter of choosing a calm spot. If you stay more than two nights, you can radio in and have the houseboat moved once during your stay. When the houseboat is anchored (and the Carolina Skiff tied up conveniently to its side), the pilot returns to Beaufort and your houseboat adventure begins in earnest, with abundant possibilities for adventures on and off the houseboat.

MAKE WAVES

Your houseboat serves as a haven and base for exploring Cape Lookout National Seashore. This low-lying narrow ribbon of sandy islands runs from Ocracoke Inlet in the northeast to Beaufort Inlet to the southwest. The barrier islands basically consist of wide and bare beaches, low dunes covered with scattered grasses, flat grasslands, and salt marshes along the sound side.

For centuries, these islands served as major fishing bases, with several self-contained communities thriving on the abundant fishing nearby. Heavily loaded fishing boats stayed on the deep water on the Atlantic Ocean side, while shallower draft boats plied the sound and maintained contact with the mainland for goods and services. The sound side of all the barrier islands also has long served as sheltered anchorage — for boats during storms (especially Nor'easters), for ships hiding from enemy submarines during World War II, and for houseboats today.

Most houseboaters choose to anchor somewhere out near Cape Lookout and the Cape Lookout Lighthouse. Shackleford Banks is separated from South Core Banks by narrow Barden Inlet, with several quiet anchorages possible on either side (depending on the wind, tides, and other factors).

This base in the shadow of the lighthouse provides easy exploration of Shackleford Banks, the lighthouse, and the even more deserted areas of North Core Banks farther north. After all of these daytime explorations, it's enjoyable to simply head back to the houseboat. Your evening can include a hot shower, a cold drink, dinner (possibly even freshly caught fish), and simply lying out under the stars. — *Lynn Seldon*

OUTDOORS

EARLY SETTLERS: A HORSE STORY

Survivors since their arrival in the early 1500s, the wild horses of the Outer Banks are part of an extraordinary breed.

WILD HORSES OF SHACKLEFORD BANKS FOUNDATION
web: shacklefordhorses.org

THE SEEMINGLY GENTLE NATURE of the wild horses at Shackleford Banks — appearing almost docile to the onlooker who is willing to keep his distance and observe in silence — belies the hardships the horses have endured.

During the 400-plus years they have roamed North Carolina's Outer Banks, the horses have survived everything from monstrous hurricanes and brutal summer heat to blood-sucking, disease-carrying insects and a less-than-ideal diet of sea oats and marsh and island grasses. About 10 years ago, 74 of the Shackleford horses — representing a huge chunk of the herd — were euthanized after testing positive for equine infectious anemia, an incurable, sometimes-fatal blood disease. Because North Carolina law requires that infected horses be destroyed or quarantined, state veterinarians euthanized the horses, deeming them a threat to the state's domestic equine population. Horse activists had argued that, because the Shackleford horses were living on an uninhabited island, they were, in effect, already quarantined. They lost that battle, but they vowed to protect the horses' future.

It quite literally took an act of Congress, but the wild horses of Shackleford Banks, which collectively have been one of our state's most popular tourist attractions for generations, now enjoy the freedom to roam their small island for untold generations to come.

SPANISH DESCENDANTS

The legislation, known as the Shackleford Banks Wild Horses Protection Act, was enacted in 1998 and ensured the preservation of the horses through a cooperative management plan to be implemented by the National Park Service and the nonprofit Foundation for Shackleford Horses.

"We think these horses are very well worth saving, because they're a part of the culture and history of this area," says Carolyn Mason, president of the Foundation for Shackleford Horses. "They are the largest genetically viable herd left of the North Carolina 'banker horses.' There are some at Ocracoke and some at Corolla, but this is the largest group left."

About 120 horses live on the small, uninhabited island of Shackleford Banks, which is about nine miles long and averages less than a mile in width. The foundation and the park service's mandate is to maintain a herd of between 110 and 130 horses, using birth control and occasional removal-and-adoption roundups to keep the herd within that range. Allowing the herd to grow much larger than 130 horses would threaten the island's ecosystem and the horses because food would become too sparse, according to Stuska.

It is an ironic projection, considering that the horses already have survived on their own for some 400 years along the Outer Banks. According to Mason, genetics testing and historical documentation indicate that the horses are descended from those brought to the coast in the early 1500s by Spanish explorers. One such explorer, for example, was Lucas Vasquez de Ayllon, who in 1526 attempted to settle somewhere along the coast of what is now the Carolinas. When the colony failed, the survivors caught a passing ship back home, leaving behind close to 100 horses.

Another theory implicates the *Tiger*, a flagship sent by Sir Walter Raleigh, which sailed to Hispaniola in 1585. The ship's commander, Sir Richard Granville, reportedly traded for or stole some Spanish horses, then sailed north and ran aground near what is now Portsmouth Island. Historians speculate that Granville and his crew may have jettisoned the horses to make the ship lighter.

By 1926, as many as 6,000 horses roamed the Outer Banks, but their ranks gradually thinned as the region became more developed. Fortunately, the horses on Shackleford Banks won't ever have to contend with developers.

— *Jimmy Tomlin*

VISITORS WELCOME

Because Shackleford Banks is part of the Cape Lookout National Seashore, which is a national park, visitors are welcome and encouraged to visit the island and try to spot the horses. But as you're planning your visit, there are a few things you should know:

- **Shackleford Banks is not accessible by car.** You can access the island by private boat, or you can take any number of public ferries to reach the island. You'll be exploring the island on foot, so sturdy, waterproof shoes are recommended. Horses roam the entire island, so you may have to do quite a bit of walking to find them.
- **The island is primitive.** There are only two compost toilets on nine miles of island. There's no drinking water on the island, no soda machines, and only one shade shelter. Take everything you'll need with you — water, sunscreen, bug spray, hat, and rain gear.
- **Remember that horses are still wild animals.** "They're used to seeing people, but they don't like to be approached too closely," says biologist Sue Stuska. "The best way to view the horses is by binoculars or a camera with a telephoto lens, and to stay about 30 feet away. You don't want to disrupt what they're doing. If they're eating and you walk up too close or you walk up too quickly, they're going to be disrupted and lose that valuable feeding time. If they're nursing and the mom leaves because you're too close, the baby loses that valuable nutrition," she notes. Feeding, touching, teasing, frightening, and disturbing the horses are all federal violations, and violators can be fined as much as $5,000 and spend up to six months in jail, says Stuska. "Don't try to pet foals," Mason adds. "A stallion's primary job is to gather mares and produce babies, and then protect those babies. You wouldn't go to somebody's yard that had a dog and puppies and just walk up and grab a puppy and not get bitten. It's the same way with the horses. Use common sense, and be aware that these animals have some right to this space, too."

LIFE IN A FISHBOWL

Stocked to the gills, the North Carolina Aquarium at Pine Knoll Shores gives visitors an up-close view of wildlife without getting wet.

NORTH CAROLINA AQUARIUM AT PINE KNOLL SHORES
1 Roosevelt Boulevard, Pine Knoll Shores, N.C. 28512
phone: (866) 294-3477 **web:** ncaquariums.com/pine-knoll-shores

HOURS/ADMISSION
9 a.m.-5 p.m. daily, year-round, closed Thanksgiving Day, Christmas Day, New Year's Day
Admission: $8, adults; $7, seniors; $6, children ages 6-17; free for ages younger than 5

AFTER A $25 MILLION EXPANSION that more than tripled the space about five years ago, the aquarium has claimed its spot as one of the premier attractions on the coast. Presenting the theme "From the Mountains to the Sea," aquarium exhibits represent the state traveling west to east, beginning with a striking mountain waterfall, spilling 32 feet into a pool, sending mist and spray into the air. A Smoky Mountain trout pool and two creek exhibits are found in the mountain gallery, and in the Piedmont gallery, two young male river otters — the only mammals among the 3,000 animals at the new aquarium — captured from the wild in Pender County steal the show. A viewing window gives visitors a look at the otters' underwater tricks — they can swim as fast as 12 miles per hour — as well as their playful antics on land, where they often slide down mud banks on their bellies.

Another standout exhibit is the 306,000-gallon "Living Shipwreck." A four-foot-long sand tiger shark and schools of fish that live around shipwrecks swim around a replica of the German U-352, which was attacked and sunk by the U.S. Coast Guard cutter *Icarus* in 1942. The replica looks much like the wreck site as it would be seen by divers off Cape Lookout, with its hatches and portholes open. Thanks to a 60-foot-long observation window and a special microphone system, visitors can hear local divers who enter the exhibit tell the story of the sharks, sea turtles, and other schools of fish swimming alongside them in the large tank. And a 50,000-gallon "Queen Anne's Revenge" exhibit gives visitors an underwater glimpse of what is believed to be the grave of Blackbeard's flagship, which sank in Beaufort Inlet in 1718. Timbers, cannons, and other artifacts have been pulled from the sandy bottom since it was discovered in 1996. Green sea turtles, nurse sharks, black sea bass, and red drum are among the fish that call the exhibit home. *— Misti Lee*

THE SANITARY FISH MARKET RESTAURANT

Fresh seafood and friendly service have been hooking
coastal visitors for years.

THE SANITARY FISH MARKET RESTAURANT
501 Evans Street, Morehead City, N.C. 28557
phone: (252) 247-3111 **web:** sanitaryfishmarket.com

HOURS
Open for lunch and dinner every day, February through November.

CAPTAIN TONY SEAMON AND TED GARNER opened the Sanitary Fish Market in 1938. Today, the well-known restaurant continues to draw customers from near and far. Each week the Sanitary serves up a staggering amount of seafood: 800 pounds of shrimp, 70 gallons of scallops, 70 gallons of oysters, and countless fillets and steaks of fresh seafood. The restaurant that originally seated 12 (at bar stools) currently seats more than 650. Chef David West, who has been with the restaurant for more than 35 years, says "During the summer, we can serve 2,000 meals a day."

When entering the restaurant, a rogue's gallery of sorts greets hungry patrons. A narrow, paneled hallway testifies to the history; photos from floor to ceiling — enough for a modest museum — trace the eatery's lineage. Among the who's who of patrons: Every North Carolina governor since 1941, sports and music celebrities, and even former president George H.W. Bush. — *Bryan Oesterreich*

EAT AND DRINK

FISH HOOK GRILL

Distinctly Down East dining makes this restaurant a return destination.

FISH HOOK GRILL
980 Island Road, Harkers Island, N.C. 28531
phone: (252) 728-1790 *web:* fishhookgrill.com

A CERTIFIED MEMBER OF THE CARTERET CATCH program, which is designed to support local seafood, Fish Hook Grill serves fresh, off-the-boat seafood with genuine Harkers Island style. Folks craving Faye Moore's tasty creations, like fried oyster sandwiches, will find them here, along with bowls of the hearty seafood chowder with cornbread dumplings that the Outer Banks food maven is known for. — *Diane Jakubsen*

THE BIG OAK DRIVE-IN & BAR-B-Q
"One shrimpburger and an order of onion rings, please."

THE BIG OAK DRIVE-IN & BAR-B-Q
1167 Salter Path Road, Salter Path, N.C. 28575
phone: (252) 247-2588

THE BIG OAK DRIVE-IN WAS FOUNDED IN 1976 by a Salter Path commercial fishing family who wanted to cook and serve their catch rather than sell it wholesale. Bobby and Elizabeth Lawrence's eatery was a big hit on Bogue Banks. The family later decided to lease the restaurant, and in 1990, Stewart Pickett, a former shoe businessman, became the proprietor.

"I had not eaten at The Big Oak before, but I heard about its reputation," says Pickett, who runs the restaurant with his wife, Janet, and manager of 16 years, Jamie Godfrey. "The food was always good, always fresh, and always plenty. I knew there was no way I could lose if I could do it just half as good."

Pickett obtained all of The Big Oak's recipes and opened the doors. Now, years later, The Big Oak is going strong as one of the most popular spots on the Crystal Coast.

Most people come for the shrimpburger, their biggest seller. It's a soft, steamed bun slathered with tartar sauce and piled with hot fried shrimp, The Big Oak's spicy red sauce, and cole slaw. The Big Oak also serves a lot of eastern-style chopped barbecue, both plates and sandwiches with all the sides. Other favorites include the scallop burger, crab cake sandwich, flounder sandwich, seafood plates, burgers, hot dogs, onion rings, hushpuppies, milkshakes, banana pudding, and apple sticks.

"Everything we sell we make," says Pickett. "It's all homemade. Well, except for the buns." — *Molly Harrison*

BALD HEAD
ISLAND
LIGHTHOUSE

IN THE AREA:
SOUTHPORT

CHAPTER SIX

BALD HEAD ISLAND LIGHTHOUSE
OLDEST TOWER IN THE STATE

ALTHOUGH ITS LIGHT WAS EXTINGUISHED in 1935, the Bald Head Island Lighthouse still draws visitors to peaceful Bald Head Island, which can be reached only by passenger ferry from Southport or by private boat. Nicknamed Old Baldy, the tower's weatherworn stucco exterior and octagon shape represent the early years of lighthouse construction.

"We love Old Baldy's historic patina," says Susan Grantier, historic tour director with the Old Baldy Foundation. "We feel like the walls tell a story, so even though it's been recommended to us by engineering experts to remove all the patches on the brick and to put all new material on it, we don't want to do that. We want to keep the stories that are told on the surface of this lighthouse."

Old Baldy is the second of three lighthouses built on Bald Head Island to help vessels maneuver past the dangerous shoals and into the mouth of the Cape Fear River. The first light, built in 1795, fell victim to erosion. In 1817, the lighthouse that stands today was built using bricks from the first one. The

HOW TO GET HERE:
The ferry to Bald Head Island leaves Southport from Deep Point Marina, located at 1301 Ferry Road, departing on the hour and departing Bald Head Island on the half hour. (910) 457-5003

• Deep Point Marina
Take N.C. Highway 211 (Howe Street) into Southport. Turn left at the light at Moore Street. Bear right at the traffic circle. Turn right into Deep Point Marina. Follow the signs for passenger departure. Ferries leave at the top of the hour. The Bald Head Island Lighthouse is a short walk from the ferry landing on the island.

WHEN YOU GET HERE:
Cars are prohibited on the 14-mile-long island. Transportation is by golf cart, bicycle, tram, or foot. Most accommodations furnish golf carts and bicycles for visitor use.

Cape Fear Lighthouse, a 159-foot skeleton tower, was also constructed on the island and served from 1903 to 1958, until the Oak Island Lighthouse on the mainland became operational.

Generations of Cape Fear families grew up with Old Baldy, enjoying picnics near the lighthouse and climbing inside the 110-foot-tall tower. "This was part of our pirate adventures," says Randy Jones, director of tourism for Southport and a member of the board of directors that oversees the lighthouse. "We'd run up and down the wooden steps. They hadn't put windows on it yet, so we'd climb to the top and go out on the ledge."

Trips onto the ledge have ended, but the lighthouse is still open. Visitors can climb 108 wooden steps to the top, stopping on several landings for a peek out a window. "We hear all the time from visitors that it's definitely one of their favorites," Grantier says. "It may not be the tallest or the most dramatic, but there's no other lighthouse like it in North Carolina." *— Misti Lee*

HOW'D BALD HEAD ISLAND GET THAT NAME?

IN THE 1700S, CAPE FEAR RIVER PILOTS stood atop the sandy hills at the southern part of Smith Island to get a better glimpse of ships heading toward the river. David Stick notes in the *Encyclopedia of North Carolina* that these hills were denoted "Barren Head" on a 1733 map; by 1770, the name had changed to Bald Head, a more descriptive — and memorable — nod to the rounded bluffs that resembled, well, bald heads.

STAY AND SLEEP

CAPTAIN CHARLIE'S I, II, AND III

Spend a weekend in a former lighthouse keeper's cottage.

BALD HEAD ISLAND LIMITED
P.O. Box 3069, Bald Head Island, N.C. 28461
phone: (800) 432-7368 *web:* Bhisland.com

LIGHTHOUSE KEEPER CAPTAIN CHARLES NORTON SWAN lived his dream life on Bald Head Island, lighting the lamp to put the new Cape Fear Lighthouse into service in 1903 and running the Cape Fear Light Station for the next 30 years. Today, Bald Head Island visitors can step into Swan's sandy shoes, thanks to three lighthouse-keeper cottages that are available for vacation rental. The three wood-frame dwellings — one which housed Swan and his family and the other two occupied by his two assistants — overlook the wide beach and were originally built in the early 1900s. When the lighthouse was deactivated in 1958, the cottages were abandoned. By the 1970s, the houses were placed on the National Register of Historic Places, and a few years ago, each cottage underwent a complete renovation. Each one was furnished with luxury conveniences like comfortable adirondack chairs for gazing at the view and stainless-steel appliances in the full kitchen.

> Each cottage comes with a four-person golf cart — the only motorized transportation — to explore the island.

Each cottage comes with a four-person golf cart — the only available motorized transportation — to explore the island. Most cottage guests quickly locate Maritime Market, a gourmet grocery and deli, about a mile down Federal Road to supply ingredients for meals at the cottage or to pick up an afternoon milkshake at the Ice Cream Shoppe. — *Lynn Seldon*

STAY AND SLEEP

MARSH HARBOUR INN

Enjoy a view of the Bald Head Island Lighthouse from a seaside retreat.

MARSH HARBOUR INN
21 Keelson Row, Bald Head Island, N.C. 28461
phone: (800) 680-8322 *web:* marshharbourinn.com

OVERLOOKING BALD HEAD CREEK and the Cape Fear River, Marsh Harbour Inn stands as one more reason to make the two-mile voyage from Southport across the Cape Fear River. The views from the inn are amazing, and not just looking out, either.

"Each room in the inn is a study in light, serenity, and relaxation," says Rod Hyson of Bald Head Island Rentals. Suite 10, the Pinnacle Suite, is a particular favorite among guests for its stunning views in all directions, according to Hyson. "The sunsets are unbelievable. You can see across the Cape Fear River and Atlantic over to Oak Island."

> Each room in the inn is a study in light, serenity, and relaxation.

Each morning, the inn provides a continental breakfast, and afternoon tea and cookies are served in the parlor overlooking the harbor. Many of the rooms also have decks to provide maximum exposure to fresh air and wide-open spaces, and if guests see something of interest from their vantage points, they can easily investigate — the inn supplies golf carts to aid in exploration.

Hyson appreciates the appeal of a low-key retreat. "Here," he says, "there are no high rises, no cars, not much of a nightlife either. ... But if you want true family time together in a beautiful surrounding with serene nature at your doorstep, Bald Head is the place." *— L.A. Jackson*

OLD BALDY LIGHTHOUSE AND SMITH ISLAND MUSEUM OF HISTORY

A tour of Old Baldy shines a little light on the history of this enduring landmark.

OLD BALDY LIGHTHOUSE AND SMITH ISLAND MUSEUM OF HISTORY
101 Lighthouse Wynd, Bald Head Island, N.C. 28461
phone: (910) 457-7481 *web:* oldbaldy.org

HOURS/ADMISSION
• After March 15: Tuesday-Saturday, 10 a.m.-4 p.m., Sunday 11 a.m.-4 p.m.
• November 27-March 15: Friday-Saturday, 10 a.m.-4 p.m., Sunday 11 a.m.-4 p.m.
• Admission: $5 adult (13 and up), $3 youth (ages 3 through 12), free for ages 2 and younger

AFTER A GOOD NIGHT'S SLEEP, the best place to explore the island's lighthouse history is in the shadow of Old Baldy, along the banks of Bald Head Creek. Here the Smith Island Museum of History is located in a reconstructed one-and-a-half-story lighthouse keeper's cottage from the 1850s.

The museum features an eclectic collection of memorabilia, including Captain Swan's pocket watch, a Lighthouse Service engineer's uniform, several Civil War artifacts, and more. From the museum, it's a short stroll to Old Baldy, where a circular wooden staircase leads 108 steps up to the lighthouse's lantern room and a great view of Bald Head Island and the entire Smith Island complex.

The nonprofit Old Baldy Foundation runs historic tours of the area. Along with entrance to the museum and the lighthouse, the tour includes a fascinating history of the island, including stories of pirates, shipwrecks, and wartime horse patrols, as well as a stop at the pilings from the Cape Fear Lighthouse and interesting anecdotes about Swan's life on the island.

— Lynn Seldon

MARITIME FOREST PRESERVE

Amid sea and sand, maritime forests shelter habitats that are
ecologically rich and hauntingly beautiful.

M. KENT MITCHELL TRAIL, MARITIME FOREST PRESERVE
Along Federal Road, east of the intersection with Muscadine Wynd

HEADING EAST on the cart path from the Bald Head Island Lighthouse,
the Maritime Forest Preserve reveals its lush canopies of gnarled shade
trees blending naturally with sabal palms. A component of the North Carolina
Coastal Reserve, the 173-acre forest is also a haven for birds. In fact, the
Audubon Society's Christmas Bird Count annually produces the highest
species count in the state, logging as many as 175 kinds of birds in one day on
the island.

The forest also contains extremely old and large trees, which protect the
undergrowth from salt spray. Don't miss seeing the 300-year-old live oak,
named "Timmons Oak," in honor of an island preservationist. Located near
the entrance to one of the island's hiking trails, the tree is registered with the
Live Oak Society because of its large size and age. The trail takes hikers on
a circular 20-minute hike through the dense forest. Two other forest trails
feature a close look at the island's flora and fauna.

Walkers can expect to see an array of wildlife, including gray squirrels,
raccoons, white-tailed deer, eastern mud turtles, black racers, green tree frogs,
Southern toads, painted buntings, Carolina wrens, cardinals, and blue jays.

The M. Kent Mitchell Nature Trail on the marsh is a boardwalk and
pathway trek through indigenous plants labeled along the way. Winding
walkers through the salt marsh and maritime forest, the trail offers an
opportunity to see green anoles, fiddler crabs, and osprey. — *Jane Paige*

OUTDOORS

BALD HEAD ISLAND CONSERVANCY

Forget souvenir seashells: A stop at Turtle Central, the Conservancy's gift shop, nets you a memorable take-home treasure and benefits a nonprofit.

BALD HEAD ISLAND CONSERVANCY & SMITH ISLAND LAND TRUST
700 Federal Road, Bald Head Island, N.C. 28461
information: (910) 457-0089 *turtle central:* (910) 457-0917 *web:* bhic.org

AS THE ISLAND'S CART PATH winds through the maritime forest, it reaches the southeastern shore that is home to the headquarters, Turtle Central gift shop, and activity center for the Bald Head Island Conservancy, a group devoted to protecting the island's natural resources. Of Bald Head Island's 12,000 acres, 10,000 are protected and will remain undeveloped.

> Summers will find naturalists leading a nightly turtle walk.

"We have a pristine environment that is not seen anywhere else," says Suzanne Dorsey, executive director of the conservancy. "This is an incredible place with a natural laboratory to learn, teach, and do research."

Summers will find naturalists leading nightly turtle walks, hands-on day camps, and kayak treks through the creeks. Guests can watch the bulletin boards around the island for schedules of numerous activities.

The conservancy campus actually includes the site of the island's third lighthouse, the Cape Fear Light Station. In addition to the tower, the station consisted of a brick oil house, three dwellings, and storehouses. This station became known as Captain Charlie's Station after Charlie Swan, the head keeper of the station for three decades. The tower was demolished in 1958, having been replaced by the automated Oak Island Lighthouse. Only its foundation remains today at the original site. — *Jane Paige*

CROQUET CLUB OF THE BALD HEAD ISLAND CLUB

Aside from the competition and social aspects of the game, Bald Head's picturesque setting is a bonus for players.

CROQUET CLUB OF THE BALD HEAD ISLAND CLUB
303 South Bald Head Wynd, Bald Head Island, N.C. 28461
phone: (910) 457-7310 *web:* bhicroquet.org

JOHN KNOTT, PRESIDENT OF THE CROQUET CLUB of the Bald Head Island Club, swings his mallet at the red, blue, yellow, and black croquet balls. "This is not your backyard game," he says, laughing. "You don't go wild, like you did playing in the backyard and sending your opponent just anywhere across the neighbor's yard. When this game is played, there is thought put into each and every move, even the ones when you 'rush' your opponent across the court," he says. (Rush is a croquet term for when your ball hits another ball across the court.)

So how did this game — which, according to legend, was started by French peasants using willow branches for wickets — end up on the lush, manicured court at the Bald Head Island Club?

A COUPLES GAME

The game officially came to the United States in 1865 with the establishment of the Newport Croquet Club in Rhode Island. Soon its popularity grew with young ladies, because it was a game they could play with their suitors outdoors. When balls were hit out into the woods, young couples would use this chance to steal away from their chaperones.

A century after croquet came to America, the game was being played by celebrities in California, New York, and Palm Beach, Florida. In 1977, the

United States Croquet Association was established, and it started setting official standards for the modern game of American Six-Wicket Croquet.

Ten years later, the Bald Head Island Croquet Club was formed through the enthusiasm and careful planning of husband-and-wife croquet team Bill and Billie Jean Berne.

"Bald Head Island was already established; the developer decided to build a court as an additional attraction," says Bill, who bought the first house here on the island. "I thought to myself, 'Now that's different' and decided to give it a try.

"It was a gradual learning experience. I didn't even know where to put the wickets," he says. The duo traveled to Florida to take lessons while the club was established. Now with 80 members, the group is one of the largest clubs in the United States.

"I think the reason we are one of the most active clubs is our focus on the training and education of the players," explains Knott. There are three ways members of the club can work on their game. The first is through a mentoring program in which experienced players are matched up with

> "I thought to myself, 'Now that's different' and decided to give it a try."

the less-experienced players. Second, to enhance education, once a week the club offers "Wednesday Wickets," starting with 15 minutes of instruction and practice. After instruction, the members hit the courts and diligently practice their shot-making skills. "Croquet College" offers a third path to learning: Formal classes include on-court skills tests.

Aside from the competition and the social aspects of the game, Bald Head Island's picturesque setting is a bonus pleasure. The courts are located in view of the long, wide beaches of the island, where a fresh ocean breeze is just enough to cool the game if the competition gets heated.

With gulls passing by and a minimum of distractions, players can easily imagine that they are playing in days gone by, when young ladies might have made a "rush" hit in order to steal a kiss behind a tree. — *Diane Silcox-Jarrett*

EB AND FLO'S STEAMBAR AND GRILL

The rhythm of island life starts with the crack of a crab
on the open-air porch of this favorite eatery.

EB AND FLO'S STEAMBAR AND GRILL
8 Marina Wynd, Bald Head Island, N.C. 28461
phone: (910) 457-7217 *web:* baldheadisland.com

FLIP-FLOPS AND T-SHIRTS ARE JUST FINE at this laid-back eatery
overlooking the harbor and Bald Head Island marina. Kicking off a
weeklong vacation? Then belly up to the teak bar for Margaritaville Mondays
and a coconut shrimp basket. Or, grab a table on the patio for great views of
boats loaded with the fresh catch, pulling in to the harbor. If the choices here
are too many, make it easy on yourself and order Eb & Flo's famous Steampot
dish, a sampler heaped with shrimp, crab, clams, oysters, potatoes, corn, and
even kielbasa. — *Elizabeth Hudson*

MARITIME MARKET CAFE

A gourmet grocery keeps Bald Head Island refrigerators humming.

MARITIME MARKET CAFE
8 Maritime Way, Bald Head Island, N.C. 28461
phone: (910) 457-7445 *web:* baldheadisland.com

THIS ONE-STOP GOURMET FOOD MARKET cures a craving for a
seaside snack. Try a Mighty Meaty Pizza or a specialty sandwich such as
an island-friendly Cuban or Lobster Roll. And to ensure your stocked beach
rental, order your groceries ahead of time, and the Market will deliver them to
your door. — *Elizabeth Hudson*

TROLLY STOP

A little stand in Southport is the top dog
when it comes to a good lunch.

TROLLY STOP
111 South Howe Street, Southport, N.C. 28461
phone: (910) 457-7017

OTHER THAN POSSIBLY AT A CAROLINA PANTHERS GAME, you won't find a better hot dog in North Carolina. First, you get a choice of four types of dogs: original (beef and pork), all beef (Sabrett), fat free (Oscar Mayer, beef and turkey), and vegetarian (Light Life Smart Dog, soy protein). You can make it any way you choose, but those in the know go for one at the top of the list — the North Carolina Hot Dog.

It comes smothered in homemade chili, slaw, and deli mustard. Other favorites include the Cape Fear (mayonnaise and cheese) and the Old Baldy (totally plain.) Ask for a 25-cent Schwartz kosher dill pickle spear, and you have yourself a meal. — *Lynn Seldon*

OAK ISLAND
LIGHTHOUSE

IN THE AREA:
SOUTHPORT, OCEAN
ISLE BEACH

CHAPTER SEVEN

OAK ISLAND LIGHTHOUSE

STRONGEST LIGHT IN THE COUNTRY

RECOGNIZED AS ONE OF THE MOST POWERFUL LIGHTS in the nation, the Oak Island Lighthouse on Caswell Beach has been warning mariners away from the dangerous Frying Pan Shoals for 50 years.

When the lighthouse was activated in 1958, it was the second brightest in the world, according to the Friends of Oak Island Lighthouse. At the time, carbon-arc mercury lamps were used in 36-inch reflectors. Although the technology is updated, the tower still uses a distinctive signal: four one-second flashes every 10 seconds.

The concrete, silo-styled tower is one of the last two lighthouses built in the country, and the only one in the state to be built by the United States Coast Guard. The eight-inch-thick walls feature a three-strip color pattern — black, white, and gray — that's permanently cast into the concrete.

The lighthouse was recently placed on the National Register of Historic Places. "Part of the reason for that is it's the only lighthouse in the world built like this," says Judy Studer, a Friends volunteer. "The coloration is embedded into the concrete so it will never have to be repainted."

The lighthouse was built within a week. The concrete tower was poured, one section at a time, then United States Marine Corps helicopters lifted the 11-foot-tall aluminum lantern housing onto the top. Since then, it has safely guided mariners into the mouth of the Cape Fear River.

As with most active lighthouses, the Oak Island light is always on at night — except for one evening in the 1960s. As Rick Johnstone remembers it, the island's power lines were being replaced, and plans were in place to run the lighthouse and the Coast Guard station on a backup generator. He and a fellow seaman had gone into Southport on liberty.

"All of a sudden the Coast Guard station truck drives up," Johnstone says. "He said the Coast Guard's generator failed to operate, and we didn't have any power. So they wanted us — me and Bill Hillger — to climb up the side of the lighthouse."

With tools stuffed into the pockets of their street clothes, the pair spent a good part of the evening slip-sliding in their slick-soled loafers at the top of the tower. A generator from Southport got the Coast Guard's radio system running and provided enough power for a small backup bulb at the top of the lighthouse. But once the men made the dark climb to the top, they discovered the bulb wouldn't work.

Without proper shoes and no safety gear, it made for a knee-knocking climb. "Eventually we got the nuts and bolts loose that held the cover and replaced the bulb," says Johnstone. "So we saved the day, and then the chief said, 'Okay boys, you can go back to Southport' — but we didn't. We went to bed." — *Misti Lee*

HOW TO GET HERE:
Take N.C. Highway 133 from Caswell Beach.

Did You Know?

HOW DID OAK ISLAND GET ITS NAME?

ON OAK ISLAND, weathered live oak trees are everywhere. Oak Island has been honored 12 times by the national Arbor Day Foundation as a Tree City USA.

STAY AND SLEEP

ROBERT RUARK INN

Relive the Hemingway-esque lifestyle of a world-renowned author from the front porch of the house that inspired him.

ROBERT RUARK INN
119 North Lord Street, Southport, N.C. 28461
phone: (910) 363-4169 *web:* robertruarkinn.com

ON APRIL 19, ALMOST A HALF CENTURY AFTER HIS DEATH, one of North Carolina's most talented and successful writers was inducted into the North Carolina Journalism Hall of Fame. But you won't find him in most classrooms, and the majority of his works are long out of print. Still, Robert Ruark has managed to endure.

Robert Chester Ruark Jr. was born in Wilmington on December 29, 1915. Although he grew up in the port city, it was the time he spent at his grandparents' Southport home that he cherished and later immortalized in his best-known book, *The Old Man and the Boy*. From that yellow two-story house, young "Bobby" followed his grandfather, Captain Edward Hall Adkins, on fishing

> It was the time he spent at his grandparents' Southport home that he cherished.

and hunting expeditions, soaking up the seasoned outdoorsman's wisdom and eventually casting the captain as the "Old Man" in his *Field & Stream* column and Southport-based books.

Under Adkins' tutelage, Ruark developed his wing-shooting and turkey-calling skills and learned how to hunt and preserve a covey of quail. He could throw a cast net, tong oysters, and catch a stringer of fish, and he mastered woodcraft to make an Eagle Scout proud.

This would-be Daniel Boone also read voraciously and graduated from New

Hanover High School at the age of 12; he entered the University of North Carolina at Chapel Hill when he was 15. Ruark initially majored in journalism to be near a pretty journalism coed. Only after he sold a story to *The News & Observer* did he see the potential in a writing career. To pay for food and books, Ruark made and sold bootleg liquor.

Ruark bounced through a string of jobs, starting off at the *Hamlet News-Messenger* then moving on to Washington, D.C., as an accountant for the Works Progress Administration. Fired for incompetence, Ruark landed a job in the United States Merchant Marine by getting into a fistfight with a ship's mate, who deemed the flinty Tar Heel tough enough for the job.

When his stint ended, Ruark returned to D.C. and earned a sports column at the Washington *Daily News*, where he targeted the owner of the Washington Redskins, a Detroit Tigers pitcher, and anyone else he could draw a bead on that would garner him attention.

> Ruark became one of the most famous and wealthy writers on the planet.

During World War II, Ruark sharpened his skills writing for *The Saturday Evening Post* and *Collier's* while serving in the United States Navy. After the war, Ruark went to work for Scripps-Howard, writing controversial but wildly popular columns and breaking major stories, including the relationship between mobster Charles "Lucky" Luciano and Frank Sinatra, who Ruark met together in Havana. His stories got Luciano deported, put Ol' Blue Eyes on the defensive, publicly denying any involvement with the mob, and earned Ruark stacks of death threats from Luciano's "associates" and Sinatra's fans.

In a short amount of time, Ruark became one of the most famous and wealthy writers on the planet. He was living in New York, drinking at the 21 Club, socializing with celebrities, and other journalists were writing about him.

Robert Ruark's prose brings to life the North Carolina coast of the early 20th century with intimate tales of winter oyster roasts, summer tent revivals, colorful locals, and the hunting and fishing he enjoyed so much. Today, several of his personal items are on display in Southport, and the Old Man's house is now the Robert Ruark Inn. While Ruark's legacy was once in question, it seems that his stories will weather like the live oaks that line the Cape Fear.

— *Shannon Farlow*

OAK ISLAND: THE MAKING OF A TOWN

Oak Island keeps as tight a focus on its year-round community as it does on beachgoers who flock here in search of a quiet summer vacation.

SOUTHPORT/OAK ISLAND AREA CHAMBER OF COMMERCE
4841 Long Beach Road, SE, Southport, N.C. 28461
phone: (910) 457-6964 *web:* southport-oakisland.com

U NOFFICIALLY, OAK ISLAND'S DEVELOPMENT BEGAN with the construction of Fort Caswell in 1826 and the arrival of the Oak Island Lighthouse and Lifesaving Station in 1889. The completion of the Atlantic Intracoastal Waterway in 1936 started the slow conversion of the island from a fox-hunting destination to a beach community. But the town of Oak Island wasn't created until much later, in 1999, thanks to a merger of the Long Beach and Yaupon Beach communities.

John Vereen, town mayor on and off since the 1980s, is proud of the town and the decisions it made. "We had a few growing pains, sure, but we have great residents and a great town staff. There are a lot of laid-back people here who are really just enjoying the life they have on this island."

The official population, Vereen says, is about 7,700 year-round, but that number can hit 45,000 in the summertime, however, and fishermen and second-home owners can spike visitation in the spring and fall.

Deciding to limit construction heights and convincing developers to donate land for public access areas are some of the initiatives that have made Oak Island what it is today. Although the height restriction was adjusted upwards by the vote of the local residents, mostly in reaction to federal requirements, Oak Island still has a 41-foot limit for structures, keeping the high-rises at bay.

The town convinced a primary developer to turn over the unused dead ends of streets at the beachfront and, as a result, now offers 68 beach access points — with parking — along the 10-mile beach.

Two large fishing piers — Oak Island Pier and Ocean Crest — invite fishing enthusiasts. For folks who don't fish, the attraction of both piers is that a stroll out to the end and back costs absolutely nothing.

Other distractions from the omnipresent crashing surf are plentiful. In addition to a miniature golf course, Oak Island sports a Par-3 and a full-size course for golfers. At 52nd and Yacht streets, on the Intracoastal side, Memorial Park offers a nature center, picnic sites overlooking the water, a small pier, and a stroll through the woods along the clever "Talking Tree Trail," which features illustrated plaques informing visitors about the trees they encounter along the trail.

Sunrises and sunsets can be more dramatic here than elsewhere.

As you might expect, the island and nearby mainland offer a range of dining experiences. Stick around for a while, though, and you may find yourself gravitating toward the restaurants favored by locals, like Russell's Place, next to the police station on Oak Island Drive. Or you may prefer a family-friendly place with a marina view, like the Fish House at the Blue Water Point Marina on West 57th Place.

Oak Island is situated differently than most North Carolina barrier islands. It lies more east-to-west rather than north-to-south, which means its sunrises and sunsets can be more dramatic than elsewhere. If you're driving the main drags of Oak Island Drive or Beach Road at dawn or dusk, the sun will likely be in your eyes. But that's a small price to pay for the benefits of living along the beach strand encapsulated in the town of Oak Island. With light, continual breezes from the ocean to temper hot days, relatively calm waves (a benefit of the island's alignment), and an average year-round temperature of 70 degrees, Oak Island may just be your idea of paradise. — *Bill Cissna*

THE BEACHES: CASWELL, YAUPON, AND LONG BEACH

The barrier island off the coast of Brunswick County indulges those who prefer quiet beaches to clattery nightlife.

BRUNSWICK COUNTY CHAMBER OF COMMERCE
4948 Main Street, Shallotte, N.C. 28459
phone: (800) 426-6644 *web:* brunswickcountychamber.org

AT 14 MILES LONG, OAK ISLAND is the longest of the Brunswick Islands, the barrier islands off the coast of Brunswick County. Long enough to accommodate the towns of Caswell Beach, Yaupon Beach, and Long Beach. A high-rise bridge sails up and over the Intracoastal Waterway and acres of lush salt marsh. Onto the island, and each community carries its own personality.

Caswell Beach is the least commercial area on the island, a community of year-round and summer homes. A low corridor of dunes and shrubbery lines the main road, which hugs the shoreline for a pleasant stretch.

Named for the yaupon holly that grows with reckless abandon, Yaupon Beach is a small community of primarily permanent residents, many of whom are retirees. Oak Island's library is located on Yaupon Beach — and so is the highest pier in North Carolina.

Fishermen have long flocked to Long Beach, and visitors who prefer not to cast may enjoy the scenic walkway, a crab dock, and canoe ramp, as well as an extensive sidewalk system that many skateboarders have grown to enjoy. The beach strand faces south, which explains gentle surf and moderate tides. Houses along the strand and waterway are of the comfortable, traditional vacation style set in natural, offhand landscaping of native shrubs and trees.

— Ede Baldridge

EAT AND DRINK

TOAST OF THE COAST

Organizing great day trips from Oak Island, wine pioneers at Ocean Isle Beach create a slice of Sonoma in the southeastern part of the state.

SILVER COAST WINERY
6680 Barbeque Road, Ocean Isle Beach, N.C. 28469
phone: (910) 287-2800 **web:** silvercoastwinery.com

HOURS
Monday-Saturday, 11 a.m.-6 p.m., and Sunday, noon-5 p.m.
During January and February, hours are Wednesday-Sunday, noon-5 p.m.

MARYANN CHARLAP AZZATO STARTED SILVER COAST Winery in 2002 with her husband, longtime Southport orthopedic surgeon Dr. "Bud" Azzato. "We love wine, and we love our coastal location, so we combined the two," she says. Inside the winery, guests receive a tour, which includes a visit to the fermentation room and the barrel room, which sets a nice mood with its stacked barrels, dim lighting, and indoor waterfall and pond.

Next, visitors taste the fruits of the labor of renowned winemaker Dana Keeler, whom the Azzatos lured New York's Finger Lakes region, a prestigious winemaking district. Eight years into its opening, Silver Coast Winery has received more than 220 medals, most won at International Wine Competitions held throughout the United States. Stay for a taste to discover the award-winning flavors for yourself.

Five bucks gets you a choice of five whites or five reds, poured by Al Gomes, Silver Coast's tasting manager. He knows his wine, and he loves directing visitors to wines they'll enjoy, like the Touriga, also called The Cape Fear Blood Wine, or the Calabash White, which is designed to be the perfect accompaniment to a plate of fresh North Carolina seafood.

— *Lynn Seldon*

YACHT BASIN PROVISION CO.

Fantastic food and a fun dining experience signal to diners that their ship has come in.

YACHT BASIN PROVISION CO.
130 Yacht Basin Drive, Southport, N.C. 28461
phone: (910) 457-0654 *web:* provisioncompany.com

THE EXPERIENCE STARTS THE MOMENT YOU PULL INTO the parking lot (or dock). Stand in a line, which occasionally goes out the door, and then order your food from the counter. The menu is on a chalkboard right inside the screen door. Once you've placed your order, grab your drinks on your own (on the honor system). The wait staff keeps track of your entire order on 3-by-5 cards, and you pay when you leave.

Veteran visitors often order the fritters or chowder as appetizers and then head back to the counter to order their main course. Favorites here include conch fritters, freshly made seafood chowder, steamed shrimp, crab cakes, a great grouper salad sandwich, and some seriously tasty hamburgers. The menu hasn't changed much since Paul Swenson and Maria Tilling opened the place in 1993. "Our menu has always been based on good, casual, and reasonably priced food," says Paul.

"We let the food speak for itself."

"It is only food. We don't try to disguise it. We let the food speak for itself," says Maria. Of course, it's only natural that seafood would play a key role. The steamed shrimp is a perennial bestseller, but the melt-in-your-mouth grilled tuna dinner, crab cakes, and fish-filled grouper salad sandwich are favorites, too.

The New England seafood chowder is one of the best you'll taste north or south of the Mason-Dixon line. The Provision Co. version includes shrimp, clams, fish, and lots of cream, but there are a few other flavors in there — a guarded secret that Paul and Maria won't reveal — that make all the difference.

The get-your-own drink system, along with the ordering and delivery of food, were all based on Paul and Maria's desire to keep things simple and operate with just a few staff members. Originally, customers wrote their own order and included their first names on the index cards. Now, orders are written down by a staff member at the counter, but first names are still the rule, and it's just one of the place's personal touches. During lunch and dinner, "organized chaos" best describes the narrow kitchen just behind the counter. "Like any kitchen, we have all developed our own routine, where insanity and practical jokes reign," Maria says. "Sometimes, for our staff meals, we add hidden treats in the food — like habanero peppers and hot sauce."

HAPPY MEMORIES

In November, the restaurant prepares for more antics with the Stede Bonnet Regatta, which started as a Halloween sailing party soon after the restaurant had opened. Normally sane sailors turn into swashbuckling plunderers, complete with massive water balloon fights and a competitive race. The awards ceremony features hilarious speeches, feeble attempts at conch blowing, and a huge buffet dinner served by Provision Co. staff free of charge. Maria, dressing the part, says, "It developed as a way to thank our loyal customers for a great year and now has a life of its own on and off the water."

Paul and Maria, long-time staff members, and restaurant regulars have lots of memories, which they are happy to repeat at the little bar. While they're both from the Northeast, they each fell in love with the Carolinas early in life. Paul went to college in South Carolina and settled in Raleigh; Maria moved to Southport after years in the Carribean. When they met, Paul relocated to Southport, and they tried to figure out something they could do together.

"We wanted to work together, combining our restaurant skills," Maria says. "We thought the waterfront was a great location for a casual outdoor dining restaurant. It's wonderful to be able to go to work in shorts, have a great view of the water, work in a profession we love, and live in a great town." — *Lynn Seldon*

TRAVEL NOTES

TRAVEL NOTES